What a waste

MANCHESTER
1824

Manchester University Press

The *Manchester Capitalism* book series

General Editor

MICHAEL MORAN

Manchester Capitalism is a series of short books which reframe the big issues of economic renewal, financial reform and political mobilisation. The books attack the limits of policy imagination in everything from university pedagogy to financial regulation. Our working assumption is that a reframing of policy choices is necessary before we can reform present-day capitalism.

Manchester Capitalism is also a group of researchers (www.manchestercapitalism.co.uk) whose work combines 'follow the money' research with political discussion of narrative alibis. Our distinctive analysis was pioneered in public interest reports about mundane activities like meat supply and railways for the Centre for Research on Socio-Cultural Change (www.cresc.ac.uk).

We write in the tradition of provincial radicalism for a broad audience of citizens because we believe there is much distributed intelligence in our society outside the metropolitan centres of elite decision making. Our work is politically challenging because it revives the liberal collectivism of Berle or Macmillan and borrows from free-thinking critics of capitalism like Wright Mills and Braudel.

The first book in our series, *The end of the experiment?*, analysed the failure of the post-1979 British experiment in state planning of competition and markets before arguing for a better way. The present book about outsourcing takes that argument further. Future volumes will extend the analysis beyond the UK.

What a waste

Outsourcing and how it goes wrong

Andrew Bowman, Ismail Ertürk, Peter Folkman,
Julie Froud, Colin Haslam, Sukhdev Johal, Adam Leaver,
Michael Moran, Nick Tsitsianis, Karel Williams

Manchester University Press

Published by Manchester University Press
Altrincham Street, Manchester M1 7JA, UK
www.manchesteruniversitypress.co.uk

British Library Cataloguing-in-Publication Data
A catalogue record for this book is available from the British Library

Library of Congress Cataloging-in-Publication Data applied for

ISBN 978 0 7190 9953 3   paperback
ISBN 978 0 7190 9952 6   hardback

First published 2015

Typeset by Servis Filmsetting Ltd, Stockport, Cheshire
Printed in Great Britain by Bell and Bain Ltd, Glasgow

Contents

List of exhibits   vii
List of abbreviations   viii

1 Outsourcing: organised money and disabled government   1
1.1 Introduction   1
1.2 From standard narratives to the charge sheet   7
1.3 The mess we're in: co-dependent government and
    sham capitalism   13
1.4 What is to be done?   20

2 Outsourcing, blame-shifting and major fiascos   27
Charge 1   27
2.1 Fiascos as problems of knowledge/problems in
    knowledge   28
2.2 'Designed' fiascos: the case of work capability
    assessments   32
2.3 Routine cock-ups   35
2.4 Takeaways for the concerned citizen   39

3 Unjustifiable profit-taking on mundane contracts   40
Charge 2   40
3.1 Profit without risk   42
3.2 Franchise gaming and walk-away   46
3.3 Contracts levered on labour   51
3.4 Takeaways for the concerned citizen   57
Notes to Chapter 3   57

4 Undisciplined outsourcing conglomerates   58
Charge 3   58
4.1 Growth and contract roulette   59
4.2 Opacity and balance sheet risk   66
4.3 Corporate reset and ongoing co-dependence   71

4.4 Takeaways for the concerned citizen 75
Notes to Chapter 4 76

5 Outsourcing specialists and the gaming of limited liability 77
Charge 4 77
5.1 The uses and abuses of limited liability 79
5.2 Veolia 82
5.3 Biffa waste management 89
5.4 Takeaways for the concerned citizen 91
Notes to Chapter 5 92

References 94

List of exhibits

3.1	Pre-tax return on sales of outsourced activities, compared with food processors	44
3.2	Pre-tax return on capital employed of outsourced activities, compared with food processors	44
3.3	Great North Eastern Railways subsidy, premium payments, profit and dividends 1996–2007	49
3.4	First Group premium profile for winning the Greater Western franchise bid	50
3.5	UK non-retired households receiving more in benefits than taxes paid	56
4.1a	G4S group turnover and annual growth rate	63
4.1b	Serco group turnover and annual growth rate	63
4.2a	G4S cash spent on acquisitions	64
4.2b	Serco cash spent on acquisitions	64
4.3a	G4S operating profit and operating margins	65
4.3b	Serco operating profit and operating margins	65
4.4a	G4S tangible fixed assets compared to goodwill	70
4.4b	Serco tangible fixed assets compared to goodwill	70
4.5	Serco's crisis and the 2014 write-downs	72
5.1	Veolia Water UK Limited net interest and tax share of earnings before interest and tax (EBIT)	84
5.2	The corporate ownership structure of Veolia Water UK Limited	86
5.3	Veolia Environmental Services UK PLC capital structure 2000–13	88
5.4	Estimate of Veolia Environmental Services UK PLC book value 2012 and 2013	88
5.5	Biffa interest charges and operating profit	90
	Appendix 1 The corporate ownership structure of Veolia Environnement SA	92

List of abbreviations

AMP5	Asset Management Plan 5. AMP5 refers to the five-year planning period for 2010–15 during which OFWAT monitored water companies' efficiency and adjusted price limits accordingly.
ALS	Applied Language Solutions
ATOC	Association of Train Operating Companies
BDIL	Beryl Datura Investment Ltd
BERR	(Department for) Business, Enterprise and Regulatory Reform
CBI	Confederation of British Industry
CEO	chief executive officer
EBIT	earnings before interest and tax
EBITDA	earnings (profit) before interest, tax, depreciation and amortisation
EFRAG	European Financial Reporting Advisory Group
ESA	Employment Support Allowance
FGW	First Greater Western
FTSE100	Financial Times Stock Exchange index of the most valuable 100 companies listed on the London Stock Exchange, as measured by market capitalisation
G4S FMS	G4S Forensic and Medical Services Ltd
GIP	Global Infrastructure Partners
GNER	Great North Eastern Railways
IFRS3	International Financial Reporting Standard 3
IT	Information Technology
NAO	National Audit Office
NHS	National Health Service
NPV	net present value
NXEC	National Express East Coast
OFWAT	Office of Water Services, the water services regulation authority
PAC	Public Accounts Committee

PFI	Private Finance Initiative
PLC	Public Limited Company
RAV	Regulatory Asset Value. RAV is the value ascribed by the regulator to the capital employed in the licensee's regulated distribution or (as the case may be) transmission business (the 'regulated asset base'). The RAV is calculated by summing an estimate of the initial market value of each licensee's regulated asset base at privatisation and all subsequent allowed additions to it at historical cost, and deducting annual depreciation amounts calculated in accordance with established regulatory methods. These vary between classes of licensee. A deduction is also made in certain cases to reflect the value realised from the disposal of assets comprised in the regulatory asset base. The RAV is indexed to RPI in order to allow for the effects of inflation on the licensee's capital stock.
ROCE	return on capital employed (calculated as the profit divided by all the long-term capital in the business – debt and equity). The ROCE is presented as a percentage and shows the amount of profit per unit (e.g. pound) of long-term capital invested in the business.
ROE	return on equity (calculated as the profit divided by the equity – as valued in the balance sheet). The ROE is presented as a percentage and shows the amount of profit per unit (e.g. pound) of equity (shareholders' funds) invested in the business. The 'book' value, i.e. the value of the equity in the accounts, is used, not the market value of the company's shares.
ROIC	return on invested capital (calculated as the profit divided by all the capital in the business – debt and equity). This is similar to ROCE but uses a measure of profits that is after tax and adds back interest charges.
ROS	return on sales (also known as the profit margin, calculated as profit divided by sales revenue). The ROS is presented as a percentage and shows the amount of profit per unit (e.g. pound) of sales revenues.
SPV	special purpose vehicle
TOC	train operating company
TUC	Trades Union Congress
TUPE	Transfer of Undertakings and Protection of Employment Regulations

VCE   Veolia Water Central Ltd
VEA   Veolia Water East Ltd
VSE   Veolia Water Southeast Ltd

Chapter 1

Outsourcing: organised money and disabled government

We had to struggle with the old enemies of peace – business and financial monopoly, speculation, reckless banking, class antagonism, sectionalism, war profiteering. They had begun to consider the Government of the United States as a mere appendage to their own affairs. We know now that Government by organized money is just as dangerous as Government by organized mob.

(Franklin D. Roosevelt, announcing the Second New Deal,
October 1936)

The common rights of ownership have disappeared. Some of them have been sold; some of them have been given away by people who had no right to dispose of them; some of them have been lost through apathy and ignorance; some have been stolen by fraud; and some have been acquired by violence. Private ownership has taken the place of these communal rights, and this system has become so interwoven with our habits and usages, it has been so sanctioned by law and protected by custom, that it might be very difficult and perhaps impossible to reverse it. But then, I ask, what ransom will property pay for the security which it enjoys?

(Joseph Chamberlain, Birmingham Town Hall Speech,
January 1885)

1.1 Introduction

This book is about a new set of problems created by the outsourcing of public services to private contractors. It is addressed to the concerned citizen puzzled by the gap between the efficiency rhetoric of the modern outsourcing industry and the reality of delivery – which is marked publicly in the media by the reporting of fiascos and practically in service delivery by cheese-paring treatment of both employees and clients. And it is addressed to the citizen baffled by the smoke and mirrors of modern accounting, especially the way the modern outsourcer manipulates corporate tax obligations in a maze of corporate structures.

To begin, outsourcing needs to be set in historical perspective. The crisis of the 1970s led to structural reforms designed to improve competitiveness and win the favour of financial markets and international agencies. One consequence was a sale of the state-owned monopolies. In the first stage, through privatisation of activities with retail customers, the central state handed ownership and responsibility for the delivery of utilities, like energy, transport and water, to the private sector. In the second stage, through outsourcing of tax-funded or tax-subsidised activities, the central and local state issued fixed-duration franchises to private contractors which initially supplied mundane services, like local authority household waste collection.

The result in Britain by the 2010s is a kind of franchise state which has long gone beyond outsourcing non-core activities, the basis for the original private-sector practice of 'contracting out' services like IT or catering. Many of the key historical functions of the central state (like the administration of criminal justice and the delivery of welfare) are now partly in the hands of private contractors. For example, in the 2010–12 period, more than £1.5bn of incarceration and justice services were outsourced, with the largest supplying contracts worth more than £100m to individual firms (Centre for Crime and Justice Studies 2013). In 2014, the outsourcing of probation services for medium- and low-risk offenders offered ten-year franchises on contracts which were nationally worth £450m a year (Warrell 2014).

The franchise state has also gone beyond the traditional model of public-sector 'procurement', where the state invited bids for the delivery of particular goods or specific services. The local state now routinely franchises large and complex bundled packages of services to private contractors. Whitfield (2014) provides an overview of strategic partnerships signed by local and other authorities: between 2000 and 2013 some £14bn of contracts were agreed, with a clear move away from discrete service contracts covering one function like IT and towards bundled contracts covering multiple services. These bundled contracts initially covered support service for education, police and fire authorities and now extend to the full range of local authority services so that some councils are becoming commissioning bodies which buy all their services from outside (usually on a profit-share basis).

The scope and extent of these changes is already remarkable with much more to come. For example, in 2013 Staffordshire County

Council entered what was then a record-breaking £1.7bn joint venture with Capita to supply educational support services across the whole county. By 2015, Northampton County Council was planning to transfer 3,850 of its 4,000 employees to four new dividend-paying service providers which would deliver all of the council's services, including social care for the elderly (Brown 2015). This 'commission-only' model is likely to be increasingly replicated in Conservative-controlled shires and urban areas.

The result so far is a 'public service industry' of private providers which the Institute for Government estimated had turnover of £100bn a year by 2011 because 'roughly £1 in every £3 that government spends on public services goes to independent providers' (Gash *et al.* 2013, p. 4). This fits with other claims (e.g. Oxford Economics 2011, p. 6) which put the value of public outsourcing at some £80bn in 2009. But these are all guesstimates of a rapidly increasing total because it is impossible to separate new-style service outsourcing from traditional goods procurement in official statistics. These show that total government spending with third parties (including local government and National Health Service (NHS), operations outsourcing and goods procurement) for 2012–13 was £187bn, of which £40bn was accounted for by central departments, £50bn by the NHS and £84bn by local government. Indeed, local government is currently the fastest area of growth, as authorities respond to expenditure cuts: at the start of 2013 'Seymour Pierce ... identified 1,789 outsourcing opportunities worth £84bn in the government pipeline', with much coming from local government (Plimmer 2013a).

Our title, *What a waste*, compresses this book's argument: that this vast and growing franchise state is socially wasteful and administratively inefficient – contrary to the promise in the rhetoric of advocates of outsourcing. That is why it concerns all citizens and explains the audience addressed in this book. What is happening should certainly be a concern of taxpayers who are getting an inferior service for their money. But taxpayers are not a segregated social group. They are citizens linked to others: they have children, grandchildren, parents, grandparents who may or may not at any particular moment be taxpayers, but whose lives are affected by outsourcing.

Citizens should be concerned because this outsourcing is not taking place in a controlled way after elected politicians and civil servants have carefully chosen between outsourced private contractors or direct public service provision by determining the 'best buy' for cost and quality on a contract-by-contract basis. Outsourcing contracts are typically announced in press releases making unsubstantiated claims about the millions that will be saved. But questions about what exactly is going on and what is finally delivered cannot be answered because contracts are usually withheld on the grounds of commercial confidentiality (House of Commons Public Accounts Committee 2014c, p. 5); and outcomes usually only receive official scrutiny when they go egregiously wrong. This excuse routinely conceals contract terms which favour the outsourcer by guaranteeing revenue or allowing walk-away without sanction. For example, in the case of the 2014 probation contracts, the Public Accounts Committee discovered a break clause which guaranteed outsourcers their profits if the contracts were cancelled after the 2015 election by an incoming Labour administration (Warrell 2014).

It is also the case that comparisons of public-service provision by state agency and private provider are inherently very difficult. Like-for-like comparisons are difficult when the shift to outsourcing often coincides with major changes in policy regime or delivery. Furthermore, from the citizen and the state's point of view, it is not sensible to consider the desirability of outsourcing within the narrow frame of individual contract value for money. The state is responsible for roundabout repercussions and has to face the costs when savings on one outsourcing contract generate increased costs elsewhere. Laid-off workers may be reabsorbed, but cuts in pay and conditions which make one service cheaper are likely in a roundabout way to increase other social costs of wage subvention through tax credits, housing benefit and such like.

Another complication is that outsourcers typically consolidate many contracts into portfolios held by sometimes imprudent and often fragile companies. Outsourcing may sustain a diverse ecology of providers but it is increasingly a field that is dominated by large players: the Cabinet Office maintains a list of just forty strategic suppliers that account for 25% of the value of central government contracting (National Audit Office 2013b, p. 5). Specialists dominate sectors like waste management where Veolia (UK), the British subsidiary of a French multinational, is the market leader in outsourced waste management in the UK. Four huge conglomerates, G4S, Serco, Capita and Atos, have established a presence across a wide range of outsourced sectors. Outsourcing is also big business for an assortment of service, consultancy and facilities management firms, like BT, Amey, Capgemini and VT Group (Department for Business, Enterprise and Regulatory Reform 2008), which are not immediately thought of as outsourcers.

These companies are different in their national and historical origins, and in the extent to which they specialise in the provision of services for the British state. Atos in the UK is the subsidiary of a large French quoted multinational, while Capita is a FTSE 100 company built virtually entirely from British outsourcing contracts with a large private-sector business. Some outsourcers are British public companies in their own right, others are subsidiaries of foreign public companies or investments for private equity or hedge funds, while a small number are subsidiaries of state-owned mainland European utilities. But all have similar investor and financial market defined priorities: they seek high rates of return combined with growth of capital value through retaining profitable contracts and seeking favourable exit strategies to manage risk and realise gains.

The cost of this incursion by financialised players is ultimately as much political as economic. *The democratic tragedy of the franchise state is that today's mainstream politicians are not protesting (or even examining) the outcomes of outsourcing but are planning to grant ever more local monopolies from which organised money can take profits (in many cases without the capital investment or revenue risk which legitimate capitalist profit).* The chapter opens with quotes from President Roosevelt and Joseph Chamberlain – both radical, non-socialist politicians – showing how an earlier generation of statesmen routinely supposed that the power of organised money should be curbed and that private interests should pay something back after claiming public rights. The modern British politician instead implies that we should thank outsourcers for their efforts because (except in the case of the NHS) they all agree with David Cameron who, in a key speech, argued that one 'principle of modernisation' is 'opening up public services to new providers and new ideas' (2011).

Our explanation for this default towards outsourcing is that the giant contractors and the state are now bound together in co-dependence; these corporates have become what we can call *governing institutions*. The aim of Thatcherite reform and New Labour experimentation was to inject market competition into public-service provision. But its paradoxical result is, in the words of the House of Commons Public Accounts Committee (2014c, p. 3) 'the evolution of privately-owned public monopolies, who largely, or in some cases wholly, rely on taxpayers' money for their income'. The franchise state which exists to award and monitor contracts at the same time strips itself of institutional resources and intelligence previously used to deliver goods and services. As outsourcing proceeds, the (central and local) state is increasingly disabled in that it no longer has the capability to deliver public services. That produces the outcomes summarised in the title of this chapter. Organised money drives outsourcing companies to game the contractual system and taxation regimes so as to take out more and put back less into the public purse; in response, a state with limited organisational capabilities has to make a virtue of this necessity.

Our language of governing institution and our notion of co-dependence owes much to Middlemas's (1979) classic study of an earlier era of co-dependence, that of 1960s and 1970s tripartism involving a partnership between the state, employers and trade unions. But in that partnership the state was the deliverer of public services, controller of the utilities and had the self-confidence of high Keynesianism. In the 1960s, the state was easily the equal of organised employers and workers in the Confederation of British Industry and the Trades Union Congress. Now in the 2010s, the corporate actors are, in practice, the dominant partners in a new co-dependence as they game institutions and tax regimes, and manipulate contract-making; the central state is at best playing catch-up when things go wrong and much of the local state lacks resources and expertise to contract on an equal footing.

All this is neglected in public debate because many of the outsourced activities are mundane or, if important, the services matter only to marginal or disreputable groups: most citizens are not aware of who runs their local leisure centre and cannot know much about what goes on inside prisons. But the failure of politicians and policy makers to protest outsourcing has become an urgent matter because the state has outsourced or is now outsourcing services which are part of what we call the 'foundational economy' in health, adult care, welfare and security. Many of these services are or will be used by most families or individuals because the foundational economy is the basis of material security and the infrastructure of civilised life for the whole population.

On outsourcing, we are all in it together and so this book is designed with the concerned, but busy, citizen in mind. This first chapter does more than give the usual introduction to themes; it provides a comprehensive but succinct summary of the whole argument and content of the book, and concludes with our policy recommendations. The reader who wants to dig deeper can go to the four subsequent chapters which present and elaborate an investigation – using a series of charges – into the way outsourcing is presently organised.

This introductory chapter is divided into three sections. Section 1.2 begins by observing that the standard arguments for and against outsourcing have a very narrow focus. It then broadens the field of the visible by examining some undisclosed issues and adopting what we call a charge sheet approach in Chapters 2 to 5. The charges are that outsourcing facilitates blame-shifting by government; allows egregious profit-taking on contracts; does not curb imprudent growth by undisciplined conglomerates; and creates new spaces for the gaming of limited liability by the predatory parents of outsourcing subsidiaries. Section 1.3 develops a new and more radical account, which first tackles the question of how we got into this mess and then explains how the result is a kind of sham capitalism. The final section (1.4) considers policies towards outsourcing, focusing on the question of what is to be done, especially if, as we argue, government is part of the problem, not the solution.

1.2 From standard narratives to the charge sheet

Research by campaign group Transport for Quality of Life (TFQL) shows that extra costs of over £1bn per year are being incurred through a combination of debt write-offs, dividend payments to private investors and various administrative and legal costs. TFQL estimate that fare cuts of up to 18 per cent could be achieved if these costs were eliminated by bringing services back within a nationally-integrated railway under public ownership.

(Action for Rail 2015)

The franchising model has enabled train companies to generate significant financial returns for the Government, played a crucial role in delivering unprecedented growth in journey numbers, and provided passengers with improved services and better value.

(Association of Train Operating Companies 2013, p. 30)

Since privatisation, journeys have doubled. The network is roughly the same size as 15 years ago. But there are 4,000 more services a day ... This is the success of privatisation. I could go on reading out figures.

(Patrick McLoughlin, Minister of Transport, at Association of
Train Operating Companies dinner celebrating the twentieth
anniversary of rail privatisation, 2013)

The first difficulty for the concerned citizen trying to make sense of outsourcing is that public actors (for and against) push well-developed standard narratives. Our task in this section is to explain the inade-quacies of these narratives and explain how this book displaces them with a combination of political scepticism and 'follow-the-money' analysis.

Trade unions and private-sector lobby groups offer competing arguments about outsourcing which appeal to pre-existing grand narratives about state and market: the unregenerate left believes in the superiority of direct public provision uncontaminated by profit; the ideological right recommends private management and market incentives as the generic devices which bring efficiency and progress. The trade unions develop a sector-specific version of the left narra-tive about extraction, while private operators make sectoral claims about benefits. National politicians (from Labour, Conservative or Coalition governments) then publicly endorse (or, at least, do not challenge) whatever claims are made by the outsourcing operators. By 2015 this stereotyped contest is symptomatic of the current British impasse: the political classes cannot concede that the policies of privatisation and outsourcing have failed in fundamental ways; meanwhile, critics want to defend or return to state provision without recognising any faults in the previous regime. The concerned citizen is too often left with the unsavoury choice between the status quo or more outsourcing.

These points are illustrated in the opening quotations which give predictably different views of the franchising of British train opera-tion to more than a dozen private companies, which run leased trains and pay rents to an infrastructure company in the form of track access charges. For the rail unions in their *Action for Rail* campaign, train franchising means deductions for dividends and extra costs of fragmentation with the supporting evidence put together in a TUC (2015) report titled 'Towards Public Ownership': the TUC aim is to bring back an integrated, publicly owned railway company like British Rail. The Train Operating Companies (2013) take a different 'count the benefits' view of rail privatisation with claims that private management has increased passenger numbers and improved service; these claims are made and evidenced in a report titled 'Growth and Prosperity: How Franchising Helped Transform Railways into a British Success Story'. The third quotation comes from a Conservative transport minister who publicly reiterates the claims of the train operating companies at a dinner celebrating the twentieth anniversary of rail privatisation. As we have argued else-where in detail (Bowman *et al.* 2013b and 2013c), the voice of the train companies grossly exaggerates their role in increasing passenger numbers and the 'Bring Back British Rail' objective does not engage the central policy issue that (under public or private ownership) there is not enough money in the fare box to pay for the existing level of service and capital expenditure.

A related difficulty for the concerned citizen is that disinterested and expert knowledge adds little more understanding because it works within a narrow frame so that most of what is interesting about outsourcing lies outside the official field of visibility. The National Audit Office (NAO) and the House of Commons Public Accounts Committee (PAC) are certainly not in the pockets of outsourcing companies or trade unions; they have produced many detailed reports on outsourcing in the past decade and continue to do so (e.g. NAO 2013a and b; House of Commons PAC 2014a, b and c). But they take a very narrow forensic view because they concentrate on fiascos or the minority of outsourcing contracts which go catastrophically wrong in terms of service delivery and cost overruns. They then explain fiascos in a stereotyped way mainly as failures of government to write the right kind of contract and monitor its operation.

Much the same focus can be found in middle-of-the-road academic literature, like the well-received book by King and Crewe (2013) which presents a series of post-1979 case studies of major government policy blunders (including outsourcing contracts such as the Private Finance Initiative (PFI) scheme for the London Underground). King and Crewe make a number of important points particularly about 'operational disconnect' or the gap between those making and implementing policy (which figures prominently in our Chapter 2 argument). But there is a technocratic illusion at the heart of their argument – that central government is well-meaning and benevolent, but lacks knowledge and control capacity. If governments are constantly searching for better knowledge and constantly failing, maybe we should start by bracketing the technocratic assumption about benevolence. More fundamentally, autopsies of exceptional failure offer a very limited view because they tell us nothing about the sources and extent of profit-making – and unspectacular dysfunction – on the much larger number of contracts that do not go wrong. In autopsies of outsourcing fiascos, the preoccupation with individual contracts also displaces attention from the firm level and the question of why, how and with what consequences outsourcing sustains giant conglomerate and specialist firms (like Capita, Serco or Sodexo) with portfolios of contracts.

The approach offered in this book broadens the field of the visible for the citizen by combining sceptical political analysis with follow-the-money accounting. The political scepticism comes from dropping the assumption that government is benevolent and altruistic: thus Chapter 2 of this book explores the ways in which outsourcing can assist self-serving government even though it leads quite predictably to fiasco. The follow-the-money analysis of outsourcing replicates methods used in our previous studies of meat production (Bowman *et al.*, 2012) and railways (Bowman *et al.* 2013b), where we could track the flow of money within a sector. For a broader study of outsourcing across many sectors, we have here applied follow-the-money analysis to what we identified as three key nodes of value extraction and consolidation: Chapter 3 considers profit from mundane contracts which do not go wrong; Chapter 4 analyses the imprudence of giant outsourcing conglomerates which hold hundreds of contracts across different sectors; and Chapter 5 considers sector specialists and, more specifically, the relations between predatory parents and specialist operating subsidiaries.

Thus, four successive chapters focus on different issues and each introduces new argument and evidence about the costs of outsourcing. The argument is framed using the idea of a charge sheet. Each chapter begins with a short statement of a charge or indictment: the chapter then presents relevant evidence and argument with the aim of convincing the reader. As explained below, Chapters 2 to 5 lay charges that outsourcing allows blame-shifting by government, unjustified profit-taking on mundane contracts, while market pressures encourage conglomerate imprudence and the gaming of limited liability by outsourcing parents. This device allows the reader to make an issue by issue judgement of the argument and evidence presented on different charges.

Charge 1: Outsourcing allows blame-shifting

If governments outsource, ministers avoid direct responsibility when things go wrong, and this is especially useful in the case of under-funded services and toxic activities. Through National Audit Office and Select Committee inquiry, blame is then re-allocated to government officials writing and monitoring contracts; major fiasco is inevitable when government abdicates in favour of private firms with poor management control.

In the standard accounts of government outsourcing, the working assumption is that government is a benevolent agency whose disinterested agenda is citizen welfare; when government lapses in its duty of care, in the standard accounts, it becomes either an innocent gull of private interests or passive victim of its own failure of knowledge and control over outsourcers. Chapter 2 presents a rather different account where government is more a dubious agency whose self-interested agenda includes the protection of the politicians and their advisors; outsourcing fits this purpose because it allows active blame-shifting so that when things go wrong it becomes the fault of the outsourcer or the relatively junior officials who wrote the contracts.

The public interest should be safeguarded by the NAO and the PAC, but they are (in line with their normal practice) overly preoc-cupied with outsourcing fiascos where service delivery fails and/or cost overruns occur. While their investigations are no doubt important and provide some accountability to Parliament, what we can learn from their many autopsies is limited, partly because these fail to distinguish between designed fiascos and routine cock-ups. In designed fiascos, government gains politically when toxic policies like disciplining welfare claimants or deporting illegal immigrants are outsourced to firms whose role is to take the blame along with the contract. Routine cock-ups arise differently when the govern-ment outsources to companies like the giant conglomerates which have limited sectoral expertise, poor internal management controls and a propensity to buy-in problems through acquisition.

Charge 2: Outsourcing contracts in sheltered mundane activities routinely covers profit-taking without risk at the expense of the taxpayer and workforce

The problem is (a) unjustifiable profit-taking in sheltered activi-ties when limited capital investment is required, and when market revenue risk is either absent or capped by provision for walk-away; and (b) cost reductions that improve margins are too often obtained by eroding wages and conditions which can undermine quality ser-vices, and save on wages in one outsourced activity at the price of increasing the social bill for wage subvention.

Chapter 3 turns to the neglected issue of what goes on in mundane contracts which do not go wrong. Our argument breaks with the standard narrative assumptions that profit is either the driver of ben-efits for citizens or inherently inappropriate in the sphere of public services. Instead we start by recognising the legitimacy of capitalist profit under specific conditions: profit is justified as the reward for capital invested or risk on the revenue line; and equally profit is justified when the profit incentive drives service improvements and/or efficiency gains.

From this point of view, outsourcing represents the failure of capitalism in its own terms because evidence shows that in many mundane outsourcing contracts, the legitimating conditions are breached. Many ordinary contracts allow profit-taking where the outsourcer invests nothing and takes little market risk, either because revenue is effectively guaranteed or the outsourcer can walk away with very limited penalties. As for efficiency gains, in many labour-intensive services, pay cuts are used as the lever of cost reduction and Labour Force Survey evidence shows that outsourcers pay less than public-sector operators in the same social sector. This is important because the net social gain is limited if lower wages must then be subvented by the state.

Charge 3: Outsourcing has created giant conglomerates which are bidding machines focused on winning new contracts, turbo-charged through acquisitions

The stock market does not discipline but cheerleads for conglomerates whose growth is risky because that requires entry into new sectors without operating competence or good judgement about what is achievable from the next bids and acquisitions. After financial crisis destroys shareholder value, corporate reset damages other stakeholders without ending the co-dependent relation between conglomerate and government.

Over the last three decades, politicians and civil servants alike have doubted the judgement of government in industrial or commercial matters, putting great faith in the judgement of capital markets to set financial objectives and discipline inadequate managements. Our analysis of the outsourcing conglomerates, like Serco and G4S, shows how misplaced this faith is: market discipline has all kinds of perverse and unintended consequences because it exposes company managements to stock market pressure for high rates of return and growth in capital values.

One of the more significant results is the giant stock-market-quoted outsourcing conglomerate, like Serco or G4S, holding hundreds of contracts across diverse sectors, often in several countries. As Chapter 4 shows, the stock market encourages acquisition-led growth and ignores warning signs in the balance sheet, until it all goes wrong. As we argue, financial crisis then results in corporate reset with a new chief executive expressing contrition for past errors; but there is no learning inside or outside the conglomerate about the limits of the business model, which continues unchanged.

Charge 4: Outsourcing which brings specialist expertise also exposes essential service delivery to financialised practices

Within these practices, the use of inter-company loans and special dividends secure private gains at social cost because they create fragile subsidiary companies. These practices involve a 'gaming' of limited liability privileges which breach the implicit contract between investors and the state which grants such privileges.

Chapter 5 shifts the focus from conglomerates to sector specialists, like Biffa and Veolia in waste, who typically have activity-relevant knowledge and skills which gives them an operating advantage. But that is nullified when investor pressure leads to the creation of corporate structures of parent–subsidiary relations which allow the transfer of cash upwards to the parent, while immuring profit within the corporate network and restricting the claims of other stakeholders including the state.

This is a social problem for two reasons. First, our case material shows aggressive leverage which loads operating subsidiaries with debt, as well as the use of inter-company loans and special dividends to extract cash and depress taxable profits. In both cases the effect is to make subsidiary firms, providing essential services, more fragile and prone to sudden collapse. Second, this extraction occurs within parent–subsidiary structures where limited liability is being gamed because a privilege originally granted for social purposes is now being used for private advantage by firms which see no obligation to pay more tax than they are inescapably obliged to do, through their enlistment in national insurance. Such predatory relations and tax-avoiding behaviours have largely escaped attention in outsourcing, even though they would be front page news if the operating subsidiary had been recently been taken over by a quoted parent.

1.3 The mess we're in: co-dependent government and sham capitalism

> The point about Capitalism and Commercialism, as conducted of late, is that they have really preached the extension of business rather than the preservation of belongings; and have at best tried to disguise the pickpocket with some of the virtues of the pirate.
>
> (G.K. Chesterton, *The Outline of Sanity*, 1927)

After charges have been laid against outsourcing contracts and corporates, there is still the question of what this criticism implies more broadly for our understanding of capitalism and democracy. The answer is tricky because outsourcing is an opportunist activity with messy, uneven results, amidst much confusion about what management can do and has done. But we would argue that there is an overall logic to the process which costs citizens because outsourcing is what happens at the intersection between the political convenience of the (central) state and the opportunism of outsourcing companies and investors.

The standard narratives of outsourcing suppose a world that always performs according to a coherent script and is often purposively controlled. Outsourcing companies and trade unions construct their competing narratives around the shared assumption that private-sector management applies its knowledge and control for good or bad purposes; the autopsies conclude that the state lacks knowledge and control which it should acquire. Our alternative is a much more material account which presents outsourcing as a disordered, extractive process which unreliably serves outsourcing companies and their investors as well as co-dependent government. At the same time, it disadvantages the taxpayer because it enmeshes service delivery in the financialised calculations of organised money.

Financial extraction by organised money is always messy: think about how private equity funds typically make most of their money from a few good deals or about how a hedge fund strategy that works in one conjuncture usually fails in the next. Outsourcing is unusually messy because it has contract and company levels, financial results from contracts are variable and often unpredictable, margin improvement usually depends on wage cuts and margins can be eroded by a cash-strapped austerity state. Here is an overview of some complications.

- Contracts offer variable (and sometimes unpredictable) profit margins and return on capital employed (ROCE) according to the specifics of time and place. Some contracts achieve high returns, while others do not; Capita has a profitable, large contract for a bundle of services with Birmingham City Council which is discussed in Chapter 3. Yet within twenty miles of Birmingham, several local councils will no doubt be paying hourly rates for domiciliary care of the elderly which are such that no agency can make a reasonable profit, however low the wages paid to carers. However, outsourcers are generally not obliged to bid or rebid for unprofitable or risky work and conglomerates can decide to exit from whole lines of business: we illustrate this in Chapter 4, with Serco's recent decision to withdraw from healthcare.

- Austerity tightening and narrower margins provoke opportunist shifting between sectors as much as exit from low-return activities by outsourcers. There is no simple general principle of margin variation because activity specifics vary; but post-2010 austerity cuts and criticism by Parliamentary Select Committees have motivated many arms of the central state to cut prices in ways which tighten margins. For outsourcers with a margin-driven view of the world, the alternative to exit is opportunistically shifting to target the local state in Birmingham or Barnet which, on large bundled contracts, has none of the expertise required to protect the citizen. For government at all levels, outsourcing presents a contradictory process of professing to seek 'value for money' while providing sufficient opportunities for profit to motivate a queue of bidders.

- Downside risk, underperformance penalties and costs of walk-away are hugely variable between contracts. These conditions are often now being tightened so that, as we shall see in Chapter 4, a company like Serco can admit that it is losing money on contracts to house asylum seekers. But again, the state's problem is that if downside risks and penalties increase, outsourcing companies will not bid, or only those with strong balance sheets will bid. Barriers to entry and exit must be kept sufficiently low to maintain a semblance of meaningful competition, upon which the legitimacy of outsourcing ultimately rests. As Chapter 3 argues, the continuing absence of serious walk-away penalties in rail ensures that the franchise bids keep on coming in for train operating contracts, where future revenue is uncertain.

- Outsourcing is mostly of labour-intensive service activities where the contractor is often reluctant to invest. The contractual framing of obligations and the possibility of growth through replication and acquisition also discourages innovation which would shift technical limits. When labour is the largest cost, many outsourcing companies concentrate on margin improvement by eroding workforce pay and/or conditions, usually by paying new hires less. Chapter 3 draws on Labour Force Survey-based research to show that private outsourcers do pay less than public providers; it also raises the question of net gains if wage cuts within one outsourced service increase the costs of subventing low wages in another state account.

- Complications arise when extraction through contract is crossed with 'load the donkey' financial engineering of the balance sheet of an outsourcing company. As Chapter 3 explains, the outsourcer's ideal contract offers a starry return on capital employed with no physical investment, or revenue risk and with returns levered on the state or labour cost reductions. But, as Chapters 4 and 5 show, these profits are often swallowed up if acquisitions have produced a swollen balance sheet in a public company which holds a portfolio of contracts of variable quality; or if predation of an operating subsidiary by the parent has resulted in a mountain of debt.

- Outsourcing companies are often under financial pressure to overreach in ways which increase risk by undermining management commitment to managing operations and savvy bidding within a sector they understand. Organised money (stock market investors, private equity and hedge funds) wants capital growth as well as high margins. Chapter 4 uses analysts' reports to show the pressure is then on companies to become unstable bidding machines with organic growth often complicated by acquisitions; it analyses the worst case outcome of a giant conglomerate like Serco with little understanding of activity specifics which was prone to disastrous ex ante misjudgement of costs and profitability.

Because of these complications, outsourcing is a financially extractive mess which almost always promises more than it delivers socially and is seldom a solution for the citizen. Contracts are a lottery for the corporations, creating double jeopardy for the taxpayer if handsome returns on individual contracts are used to prop up the balance sheets of over-extended and fragile companies; attempts to insist that the private sector takes risk either deter bidders (and results in in less competition), divert bidders into other activities or exclude smaller third sector players that lack the size and scope to shoulder such risks. Individual contracts do not take account of roundabout repercussions like the costs to the public purse of subventing lower wages. The underlying problem is that the outsourcing contract is a device which connects the state with financialised providers which often enter bidding processes without understanding what is involved and may have little concern about what they leave behind when the contract ends.

Against this background, the concerned citizen might expect to see a slew of reports recommending that outsourcing be slowed and halted at least in specific sectors, along with the commissioning of research into outstanding issues like indirect social costs and financial engineering. Instead, we have individual news stories about how the state takes back contracts or outsourcers walk away after being defeated by complications; the stories typically report the excuses of the players and the allegations of the NAO and PAC but provide no basis for judging the standard excuse that (unexpectedly) this specific contract tuned out to be mission impossible and/or was derailed by external events. As this book was being written, the government took back the Sellafield nuclear clean-up contract (Pickard and Adams 2015; Syal 2015) and Circle Healthcare walked away from its contract to run Hinchingbrooke Hospital (BBC 2015a). Yet, overall, outsourcing continues with apparently unstoppable momentum.

In explaining this momentum, we would emphasise the political drivers behind what G.K. Chesterton would have called 'an extension of business' by private companies into hitherto off-limits, directly state-organised activities. Underlying conditions ensure that both sides have little alternative to persisting with a process that neither party controls, and which is not consistently rewarding for either. A mentality of TINA (there is no alternative) prevails because the extension of outsourcing does, on balance, serve the political convenience of the (central) state and the financial opportunism of the outsourcing companies; both parties are embarrassed actors under pressure from external expectations that do not recognise structural constraint on their ability to deliver higher financial returns or more services. The position in local government since 2010 is even more overdetermined because local government gets 75% of its funding from the centre, whose austerity cuts make some combination of local service cuts and outsourcing irresistible. All this can be witnessed in two observed forces:

1. *The convenience of the (central) state which benefits from the blame-shifting and the immediate labour cost reduction which outsourcing can deliver.* Successive governments in high-income countries have been under electoral pressure to deliver more of everything during the 'long boom' and the 'great moderation' – the sustained periods of economic growth that lasted up to the 1970s and more modestly from the mid-1990s to the great financial crisis of 2007–08. In the British case, this is complicated by the post-1979 introduction of structural reform which did not secure productive renewal, but instead created an unbalanced and unproductive economy where GDP growth depended on equity release from house prices (Ertürk *et al.* 2011). This created problems for the Treasury in managing the contradictions as flexibilised labour markets created long-term unemployed and a new need for low-wage subvention through the benefits system, while at the same time the tax base was being

reduced by pro-enterprise low-taxation rates on income, wealth and profits. Successive chancellors addressed the contradiction by a whole series of different expedients involving switching between capital and income to boost current consumption. Thus the state used North Sea oil revenues to support current government expenditure, sold assets like council housing and state-owned utilities and incurred debt liabilities under the PFI programme to finance new schools and hospitals. For other government departments, outsourcing represented an opportunity to abdicate responsibility for service delivery to private interests that make an ambiguous economic promise to do it better and cheaper, and can be politically blamed if it goes wrong. Abdication is the right concept here because outsourcing government can avoid struggle with organised public-sector workers, with the bonus that it no longer carries the can for service delivery if the private contractor can be blamed.

2. *The opportunism of the private sector which benefits from the local monopolies in new sheltered sectors which outsourcing can deliver.* British public companies (and private equity investments) are under capital market pressure for financial returns which are difficult to achieve in competitive product markets. The position is complicated in the UK by the collapse of the national manufacturing sector (Froud *et al.* 2011). After being defeated in the internationally competitive sectors, British corporate management's success was in chain retail operations, often dependent on imports and driven by consumer activity. Government action through privatisation greatly increased the size of the available sheltered sphere and outsourcing was the next step in enlarging the sheltered reservation for management and organised money. Opportunism is the right concept here because opening the gates to a larger, sheltered economy created opportunities for corporate management under pressure from organised money which wanted high returns. Thus Serco and Capita replaced ICI and GEC in a new outsourcing sector which the Confederation of British Industry now represents as 'a Great British Success Story' (CBI undated).

These two forces imply that outsourcing can be practically defined as what happens at the intersection of the politically motivated abdication of government and the financially motivated opportunism of organised money and its managers. This relation of co-dependence explains why it is so difficult to stop the advance of outsourcing on the grounds that things are going wrong, because things going wrong for somebody else is part of the design. It also explains why the value for money question of whether outsourcing is cheaper (and if so whether it is at the expense of the workforce) is practically irrelevant to the continuation of something which, by default, creates private profit opportunity and is politically convenient. Citizens should fear such co-dependence in a game that must be kept going regardless of performance or outcomes: if conglomerate and specialist firms depend on soft government contracts, crony networks are likely to become ever more important in determining who gets and keeps such contracts.

The end result is already a kind of sham capitalism. It looks like capitalism because there is competition for the market by bidders, overseen by central and local government ostensibly pursuing value for money and risk transfer. But it is a sham which covers the sale of local monopolies to private firms – a small number of which have near unassailable competitive advantage from scale and win disproportionate amounts of business – by a co-dependent government which can only keep the show going by *not* pressing value for money or risk transfer. The private-sector hope is that this can be sustainably lucrative because of the financial asymmetries central to standard outsourcing business models. The private operators are only clipping pennies in the pound on sales revenue; many outsourcers are getting no more than 5% profit margin and in many centrally outsourced activities margins are declining or under pressure. But clipped pennies can generate big lumps of profit if the outsourced sales volumes are large; and if there is no capital investment required or revenue risk, this is uniquely attractive business. The only practical problem for management is then how to manage the fund investors' requirement for growth without imprudence that crashes the firm.

This sham capitalism defeats democratic control of the economy, undermines the institutions of responsible capitalism, diminishes the supply of decommodified public goods and generally fragments the economy. Democracy is defeated because the local monopolies are granted by a state whose sovereign capacity is weakened both by its endless compromises with those who hold the franchises, and by its requirement to keep the game going. The practical economic cost is considerable. Institutionally the cost is the degrading of the public service corporation and the abuse of the public limited company. Outsourcing shrinks the sphere of public service and obliges the public provider to compete on cost, while organised money now takes limited liability and tax relief on debt and arbitrages both for the private advantage of parent investors. Substantively, the cost is a fragmentation of the economy with ever more toll booths for organised money, and a multiplicity of profit centres pursuing returns for investors regardless of chain connections across the sector or roundabout consequences. In historical perspective this is deeply ironic because organised money pursuing high returns through contracts in the 2010s is a much more disruptive force than organised labour pursuing higher wages through bargaining in the 1970s.

What's different about all this is a new hypocrisy because private investors and management routinely use the enterprise rhetoric of competition and markets while seeking monopoly niches. That is the democratic tragedy which we referred to at the beginning of this chapter. But it is not enough to lament a tragedy: we must find our way out.

1.4 What is to be done?

In our time, the curse is monetary illiteracy, just as inability to read plain print was the curse of earlier centuries.

(Ezra Pound, *Guide to Kulchur*, 1938)

By adding political scepticism and monetary literacy, we have broadened the field of the visible to show that the problems with outsourcing are fundamental and deeply seated in our governing institutions. The implication is that government, corporations and organised money will resist serious policy reform while offering what they consider to be tolerable concessions. So it is important to envisage policy changes and intervention at two levels: first, to recognise the mess we're in is such that citizens need a new framework around outsourcing which sets limits on the extent of outsourcing and deters financialised providers from bidding; and also to recognise that the immediate task is one of mobilising citizens to work around the political constraints on effective reform and make demands which start change and generate momentum.

When the outsourcing process is uncontrolled and the problems are gross, the first step in serious reform would be to set regulatory limits which block some outsourcing and require some re-sourcing. So, here are three basic prohibitions which would limit the power of government to continue outsourcing in ways which disadvantage the citizenry.

- The large-scale outsourcing of large bundles of services by local authorities (including city regions and regional governments) should be prohibited. On the evidence from Birmingham, Barnet and elsewhere, local authorities lack the capacity to deal as equals with outsourcing contractors like Capita and Serco. This is important because some tightening of the terms of central government contracts is at present being countervailed by an opening of new profit opportunities in local government contracting.

- The outsourcing of politically toxic activities like border control or welfare cuts should be prohibited. It is important that national government is directly accountable through parliamentary channels for what it does in these areas, where the buck should stop with the senior civil servants and ministers responsible for internal affairs and social security. There is endless discussion of whether and how we can encourage increased participation to redress the democratic deficit; a constructive first step is to ensure civil servants and ministers are responsible for what matters to the citizenry.

- The complete outsourcing of any activity should be prohibited. Under no circumstances should all the care homes or all the waste management be outsourced because, in such cases, the government is disabled because it loses operating knowledge and capacity. Such knowledge is doubly essential: first, because public operating knowledge of specific activities is a basis for contracting with outsourcers; second, because state operating capability is essential if outsourcing is to be a reversible experiment.

After such measures were introduced, private outsourcers would still be responsible for the delivery of many public services; and here our recommendation is that the framework of reward for service should be changed so as to deter bids from financialised providers. This proposal follows from our argument, in Chapters 3 to 5, that the problem is not the profit motive per se in public service provision. Rather, the problem is the pursuit of profit by organised money in and through companies which are the agents of fund investment strategies that undermine the most basic social delivery objectives of quality service and ready availability at reasonable cost.

These public service delivery objectives have definite preconditions, which include continuity of operation to build organisational culture and activity-specific expertise, as well as a financially robust business model which should (if activity specifics allow) fund investment and withstand downturns and other vicissitudes. However, under pressure to deliver financial results, the outsourcing conglomerates and specialists in their different ways undermine these basic conditions. As we argue in Chapters 3 to 5, the conglomerates pursue growth regardless of incompetence and accumulating balance sheet risks, while the specialist outsourcers bring income forward by stripping cash and assets from subsidiaries operated with an eye to exit. The result is ramshackle, imprudent conglomerates and/or hollowed out specialist subsidiaries.

If regulation of outsourcing should aim to hinder organised money and its extractive business models, the puzzle is how to do this. Financialised players will game most kinds of regulation and respond in ways which frustrate regulatory intent, as they do in banking. For example, if government imposed financial penalties on bids from over-extended conglomerates, then some rearrangement of corporate structures or balance sheets could be used to comply with the requirements. In this case, our recommendation is for deterrent regulation which would work by creating a less attractive habitat for organised money and its corporate agents.

- The simplest way of deterring organised money is by spoiling the profit opportunity in outsourcing. This could be done by offering outsourcing contractors a relatively small and fixed fee for management services rendered in a specific activity (after open book accounting of other labour costs). This reward fee would effectively cover management salaries and the sanction would be loss of management contract.
- This 'fee for service' regime would attract professional partnerships, not-for-profits and family firms with sectoral expertise but not giant corporates and fund investors who could not easily find a surplus over management salaries. It would promote arrangements as on the East Coast main line from 2009–15, which hired a team of experienced managers to run the trains in return for the salaries they drew.
- The logic of this is that the state, which can borrow more cheaply, would often be responsible for capital investment and would own facilities like care homes or leisure centres which were privately operated. The private management team would pay rents and (where possible) remit surpluses to the central and local state.
- In financialised outsourced activities with fixed capital requirements, like care homes, it is routine to set things up so that there is a property company and an operating company. We are here suggesting that this kind of arrangement could be used to some social purpose right across important areas of the economy.

These changes would require a rethinking of risk transfer because outsourcing, as it exists, rests on the assumption that outsourcing contracts should transfer risk from state to private operator. In our view this assumption rests on confusion and creates conflicts and constraints.

In most outsourced activities, the basic risk is that, after twenty years, society ends up with a configuration of facilities (acute hospitals, young offender prisons etc.) which is unsuited to current needs: this risk should properly stay with the state and cannot easily be laid off to the private sector whose ideas of risk are constructed around losing money. It is possible to write outsourcing contracts which shift operating risks on to bidders who may, for example, be obliged to provide services like domiciliary care for a fixed period of time in a territory, even if the service is loss-making. The problem is then that this narrows the field of bidders to those who have the balance sheet resources to take risks on a portfolio of contracts; and that would exclude most small and medium-sized private firms, as well as not-for-profit organisations.

We are, of course, far from a world where any mainstream British political party would countenance safeguarding the citizen through this kind of re-regulation, which would set limits on the extent of outsourcing and deter financialised providers from bidding for contracts. As we have argued, government (central, local and regional) has become part of the problem, is politically co-dependent on corporates and organised money and already lacks in-house competence to take back many activities. Even if government had some appetite for standing up to corporates, reform would be slow because outsourcing has entrenched vested interests which will resist change with trade narratives and lobbying, while those with contracts have legal rights and advisors to take advantage of procedure. Outsourcing may be about a clip of pennies in the pound but it is a business model for return on capital that will be defended.

All this is dramatised by the defensive manoeuvring of giant outsourcers and central government in response to skirmishing around recent political demands for more transparency and accountability which come from Parliamentary Select Committees and other mainstream critics of outsourcing. Ideologically unable to contemplate a regime of limits and deterrence for financialised providers, they ask for more transparency and accountability through disclosure and watchdogs. The interesting point is then the response of the corporates and central government (Plimmer 2015b).

The major conglomerates are carefully conciliatory. G4S insists 'we would not support moves to restrict or impede the scrutiny of any supplier'. In 2014, the four largest outsourcing conglomerates –

Atos, Capita, Serco and G4S – deflected demands for disclosure by offering open book accounting (which, as they told the PAC, they already follow in many cases); thus margins on government contracts would be disclosed, but contract terms about incentives, break clauses, compensation and such like would remain confidential. By 2015, central government had taken a much more controlling position. In a letter to major outsourcers, the chief commercial officer at the Cabinet Office insisted that 'government will be a single point of contact for public enquiries relating to the performance of privately delivered services they oversee' (Plimmer 2015b); and individual contracts would henceforth contain commercial confidentiality clauses which could prevent disclosure of margins, pricing and business plan.

Against this background, the curbing of outsourcing requires a new kind of coalition for change which enlists normal citizens and civil society organisations in protest and for an alternative. In our view, the mobilisation of social forces should not have its focus as being against outsourcing but instead should work for a new and positive vision of the importance and potential of public services. The public-sector activities being outsourced may be mundane but do matter greatly to citizens; and such activities can and should be improved by social innovation to benefit citizens. Incidentally, this means going beyond Manichean thinking and opposed stereotypes of the proper role of state and market. On the one side, market ideologues, private interests and lazy politicians argue that outsourcing is the competitive solution; on the other, a defensive coalition led by unions and professional groups defend existing forms of state provision. Neither of these positions explain adequately why public services are both important and need innovation.

The first step here is to move beyond the idea that what matters is an economy of competition in tradable goods and services that generates income, and the realisation that outsourcing is taking place in another foundational economy of basic services which determine security for individuals and society. On this basis, it is then possible to challenge technical ideas about innovation and see that what society needs is a more social kind of innovation which improves the quality and availability of foundational goods. We have introduced these ideas elsewhere (Bentham *et al.* 2013; Bowman *et al.* 2014) and will now summarise our argument.

The foundational economy produces goods and services necessary to everyday life, consumed by all citizens regardless of income or status, distributed by branch and network according to population and typically sheltered and politically franchised. The activities (public and private) include health and education; care and welfare; pipe and cable utilities; transport; much retail and hospitality. These activities are important in themselves and as the infrastructure of civilised life.

- Foundational activities account for 35% or more of employment in every region of the UK: 25% or more work in state-provided or state-funded health, education and care. (Largely outsourced) adult care alone employs 6% of the British workforce, almost as many as the 8% in manufacturing, where the largest sub-sector by employment is food processing.
- Foundational activities are mundane but crucially important because the availability, quality and cost of the basket of foundational goods (housing, utility services, food, health and social care, education) determines material security and welfare. What's in the basket is more important than minor changes in consumer income that do not secure fundamentals like fast rural broadband or care for the elderly, which require social organisation.

Equally important, the definition of infrastructure and innovation has been narrowed by mainstream economists. The result is a preoccupation with how state-funded education and transport improvements can boost the private sector, and a fetishisation of technical productivity gains even though the income gains from productivity increase will be captured by upper-income groups. It is striking that the bottom 20–40% of British employed households have gained nothing from the labour market since the 1980s. Hence the need for a much broader social definition of infrastructure and innovation where the foundational achievements could include, for example, not only rebuilding care homes but developing new kinds of community which would break down the physical segregation of the elderly.

From this foundational point of view, we could mobilise opposition to outsourcing because it actively disorganises foundational activities and inhibits social innovation.

- The state has been outsourcing core activities on an overly narrow calculus about directly saving costs (usually labour costs) for providing a specific service like incarceration or probation, without regard for levering improvements in the security and welfare of users, the workforce or citizens more generally.
- The logic of the franchise state is fragmentation by territory and the cherry-picking of territories in activities where regional and

national provision of networks and branches needs to be socially planned. Within this frame, profit seekers will then try to fragment activities in a secondary way by erecting toll booths wherever they are allowed. In railways, for example, ticketing has become a source of profit for the online ticket seller thetrainline.com, currently owned by the private equity firm KKR.

- Social innovation is not naturally part of the agenda of margin-driven contractors who are either fund investors or responsive to their needs. Such contractors are usually constrained by the specific terms of their contract and have a keen interest in reducing labour costs, avoiding investment and passing on expense so that workforce and citizens lose.

Meanwhile, thoroughgoing reform is hypothetical because, for the foreseeable future, concerned citizens will have to live with outsourcing dominated by large corporates which will be defended by local and national politicians. Thus, as an interim measure, we need a general policy of raising 'the social ask' of all larger firms and organisations (private and public) which provide foundational services and are grounded by the requirement to serve demand distributed according to population. We need to pose a modern version of Chamberlain's question at the head of this chapter: what will you give in return for the privileges offered you by the modern state? The *social ask* would be varied according to the activity and locality and might include local and regional procurement or employment/training on the supply side; in outsourcing, this would require pre-contract discussion of the chain effects and social implications of the outsourcer's business model; and the contract would then contain social clauses on employment conditions and social provision.

Outsourcing companies should be pressured by local and regional government and treated like mining companies in the Global South which are routinely obliged through social licensing to formalise what they are doing in return for concession. Compared with a limit-and-deter regulatory approach, this social ask approach would be a clumsy, slow way of curbing the excesses of outsourcing. But, when politicians drag their feet, it is something which concerned citizens in civil society can campaign for and extract concessions on. At the same time, such campaigns would raise consciousness about how the co-dependent and complacent state is as much of a problem as the big corporates.

Chapter 2

Outsourcing, blame-shifting and major fiascos

> **Charge 1: Outsourcing allows blame-shifting**
> If governments outsource, ministers avoid direct responsibility when
> things go wrong, and this is especially useful in the case of underfunded
> services and toxic activities. Through National Audit Office and Select
> Committee inquiry, blame is then re-allocated to government officials
> writing and monitoring contracts; major fiasco is inevitable when govern-
> ment abdicates in favour of private firms with poor management control.

The disruption at King's Cross and Paddington after Christmas was
totally unacceptable. Passengers deserve a reliable rail service, they
deserve clear information, and they deserve rapid help when things go
wrong. I am sorry that in this case they did not get those things ... I and
my officials were ... not, however, involved in planning for the operational aspect of the works programme or the contingency planning. That
is as it should be. Network Rail is an operationally independent body and
it needs to be able to get on with its job without political interference. If it
gets things wrong it will be held to account. We have made it clear to the
company that we expect it to deliver the outcomes for which it has been
funded over the current control period.

(Patrick McLoughlin, Minister for Transport, 2015)

Here is primary blame-shifting at work in the case of a minor fiasco.
Railway maintenance work scheduled for the Christmas break in
2014 had overrun so that passenger services were disrupted into the
New Year. But the rail infrastructure is maintained at arm's length
by (nominally independent) Network Rail with services franchised
out to train operating companies. So the transport minister was
able to blame Network Rail and harrumph in the Commons about
'completely unacceptable' failures. If British Rail still existed, the
transport minister would have had to take responsibility as health
ministers still do for NHS failures.

The process of blame-shifting becomes more complex in the case of the major contract fiascos. These preoccupy the media and political classes to the exclusion of almost everything else about outsourcing. In this mainstream framing, outsourcing contracts become an issue about everything from the brutal treatment of asylum-seeking detainees to the inept disciplining of welfare benefit claimants to the mismanagement of security at the 2012 London Olympics. Here the National Audit Office and the House of Commons Public Accounts Committee are brought in to produce reports which are independent, in the sense that they are not self-serving like the transport minister's excuses about disrupted rail services. Instead these reports play a secondary role in re-allocating blame in an entirely stereotyped way. They criticise government for lack of knowledge and competence, without questioning the policy of outsourcing and without addressing the fundamental structural problems created by an entirely unrealistic distinction between strategic decision and operational delivery.

2.1 Fiascos as problems of knowledge/problems in knowledge

There never was a golden age of government without fiascos. We should not idealise the past before outsourcing was invented because, when the British state directly delivered services (now outsourced), the state did not always deliver them efficiently or effectively. Ever since government has had the capacity to mobilise resources for grand projects, some of these projects have gone wrong in ways which can be labelled as fiasco because expenditure of money and effort is wasted and results are disastrous.

The long history of policy fiascos on the part of British central government has been well documented (for instance, Dunleavy 1995; Moran 2001; King and Crewe 2013). And major government fiascos have generally been seen as a problem of knowledge. The most popular academic account of recent British fiascos is provided by King and Crewe in a book entitled *The Blunders of our Governments* (2013). In Webster's Dictionary, a blunder is defined as 'a gross error or mistake resulting from stupidity, ignorance or carelessness', so, by implication, King and Crewe's fiascos are caused by an absence of knowledge. The most elegant academic account of twentieth-century fiascos – from Soviet collectivisation to compulsory villagisation in Tanzania – is provided by Scott (1998) who blames the high modernist attempt to control a rich world with thin knowledge: thus in Scott's thought-world, the problem is that policy makers work with the wrong kind of knowledge.

As we have argued in Chapter 1, outsourcing amounts to much more than a technical change in the way government delivers public services; it creates new governing institutions responsible for performing core functions of the state. What is going wrong therefore is more a problem *in* knowledge than a problem *of* knowledge. The fundamental problem is that old-style public administration has been displaced by a two-part managerial ideology that has shaped the core executive's organisation and limited its ability to learn from fiascos since the mid-1980s. This managerial ideology starts by distinguishing policy strategy from delivery and then recommends that the core executive should delegate or contract policy delivery. Within this frame, if things go wrong, the fault must lie with the core executive which has failed to exercise appropriate control.

Large-scale outsourcing since 2000 is only the latest manifestation of a movement to disentangle the policy-making core executive from the details of policy delivery (which has, with austerity cuts since 2010, now been extended into local government). That movement has its origins in a managerial ideology which originated in the 1980s as a response to critical analyses of 'overloaded government' which drew on earlier American business school ideas about strategy formation and head office function in multidivisional companies.

The perception was that the central state was overloaded with policy delivery responsibilities and that the senior managerial elite in the core executive – the senior civil service – lacked the skills required to deliver services on the ground or the time to think strategically. The fix was a new model of policy delivery which rested on a distinction between the two domains of policy making and delivery: policy making and advice was properly the domain of ministers and senior civil servants in Whitehall who were ill-equipped to deliver services, while policy delivery should be the job of contracted agencies, whether private or public, governed by service agreements with the contracting department. The result was the *Next Steps* report of 1988 and the subsequent reforms which laid down a pattern for the new generation of executive agencies (Jenkins *et al.* 1988). By 2012 there were over 180 agencies controlling over £30bn of public spending. The principle behind outsourcing – that service delivery should be governed by a contract between a public authority and an institution responsible for delivery – has thus dominated the wider organisation of the public sector for almost thirty years. Indeed, some of the original executive agencies – like the Stationery Office – have morphed into firms with commercially outsourced functions, while the private-sector outsourcing specialists have simply inherited the framing of policy domains which justified quasi-autonomous executive agencies.

The managerial ideology of separating policy from delivery has, from the beginning, been immunised against failure. The standard explanation for failure is that, if an executive agency or outsourcing project fails, then the problem is not the policy of delegation but imperfect and incomplete execution and the solution is always more intelligent government and more competitive markets. In our view, this defensiveness is bound up with the logic of a constitutional revolution whose reversal is politically unthinkable and practically very difficult. The revolution has created new governing institutions in the giant outsourcing firms which are bound in relations of co-dependence with the central institutions of the state and are increasingly indispensable to local government. In these circumstances it is hardly surprising that successive fiascos are met with increasingly desperate efforts to make the system work and to lay off blame on to weak surveillance of the franchise system. To do otherwise would be to admit that the new economic constitution created by outsourcing is pathologically dysfunctional and unreformable by the core executive. It is much easier to recommend a more powerful surveillance and control machine in the centre at the relevant ministry or the Cabinet Office.

The end result is perversity. The state acts as if intent on learning from failure, but this is a non-learning state. It has the apparatus of independent inquiry and scrutiny of the executive by agencies charged with allocating blame. Outsourcing is scrutinised post hoc by the National Audit Office and in hearings prompted by NAO reports conducted by Parliamentary Select Committees, in particular the House of Commons Public Accounts Committee. But the end result is stereotyped reports where the names of the failed projects change while the analysis of execution problems is the same. The NAO and Parliamentary Select Committees conduct a kind of duet which has two recurrent motifs: first, outsourcing projects are failing because of government failures to write and monitor contracts with sufficient competence; and, second, projects are failing because markets are not working with sufficient competitive rigour. The reports re-allocate blame by concluding that problems with outsourcing reveal great deficiencies in the way government in the UK is organised, in the quality of intelligence available to governing institutions, and in the quality of personnel recruited by government. Outsourcing, on this account, can work, but it depends on two conditions: freely competitive markets, and a powerful and intelligent state capable of reconfiguring the real economy so as produce those markets.

On the part of the NAO, this process of non-learning culminated with the publication in 2013 of two reports: *Managing Government Suppliers* (NAO 2013b) was designed to examine how the core executive, especially the Cabinet Office, organised itself so as to secure maximum value for money from the contracting process; *Deciding Prices in Public Service Markets* (NAO 2013c) accepted the principle of contracting for the delivery of services through market competition and aimed to develop the principles that would ensure the smooth functioning of these markets. It was not complacent about markets. On the contrary, its starting point was this:

> Markets present opportunities for services to become more personalised, responsive, efficient, diverse and innovative. They also present new challenges for government; specifically the risk that having established markets in public services, departments and local authorities may lack the capability to ensure that they operate in the interests of the users and the taxpayer, rather than in the interests of the providers whose profits are funded by users and taxpayers.
>
> (NAO 2013c, p. 4)

Managing Government Suppliers examined how the core executive can be organised to meet these challenges. It observed that:

> There is a risk that the Cabinet Office's ambitions for the centre of government are not matched by the right resources, capability and information. Taking on more responsibility at the centre creates an obligation to perform. The Cabinet Office does not currently have the right resources in place, with gaps in commercial experience and expertise below senior levels. This has restricted the extent to which the Cabinet Office has been able to build industry knowledge, and limited its credibility with departments and suppliers, who tell us that their working level contacts do not fully understand their operating environment.
>
> (NAO 2013b, p. 13)

The solution then becomes plain: the core executive, especially the Cabinet Office, must acquire the administrative muscle and intelligence needed to shape outsourcing markets according to the principles of free competition.

In their inquiries prompted both by NAO oversight reviews and NAO investigations of particular fiascos, Parliamentary Select

Committees have pursued these two themes of incompetent writing of contracts and the need to make markets in outsourcing more competitive. This, for example, is the summary verdict of the House of Commons Public Accounts Committee on the state of contracting in 2014:

> Government is clearly failing to manage performance across the board, and to achieve the best for citizens out of the contracts into which they have entered. Government needs a far more professional and skilled approach to managing contracts and contractors, and contractors need to demonstrate the high standards of ethics expected in the conduct of public business, and be more transparent about their performance and costs ... There is significant scope for government to improve its approach to contracting for public services. The Cabinet Office told us that there is a long way to go before government has the right commercial and financial skills to manage contracts and it needs to use the full range of powers at its disposal.
> (House of Commons Public Accounts Committee 2014c, p. 3)

Out of these accounts comes a utopian vision of inspection and competition: one where the messy realities are replaced by an imagined world where public officials are endowed with superb knowledge of how to write and monitor contracts, and contractors are obliged to subject themselves to the rigours of the competition. It envisions the ideal outsourcing system as akin to a Benthamite panopticon, where the state is pictured as an omniscient observer of, and controller of, markets. When this Benthamite vision is not realised, blame is allocated either to 'incompetent' public servants or to incompetent and/or venal outsourcing firms.

2.2 'Designed' fiascos: the case of work capability assessments

If scrutiny of the core executive outsourcing policies by the NAO and Select Committees is generally ineffective, the core executive itself has no incentive to learn where it benefits from its mistakes. This is so in the case of what we call 'designed fiascos' where government can outsource toxic policies. Blame-shifting has of course always been an inescapable part of the culture of higher administration in Britain: in the story books, American entrepreneurs can fail repeatedly but, in British administration, civil servants and politicians are damaged by association with major failures. In political science, strategies of blame-shifting have been well documented by Hood and his collaborators (Hood 2002; Hood and Rothstein 2001). But Hood mostly examines blame-shifting in a narrow sense as a matter of the different strategies available to actors faced with responsibility for failures. Our focus in this section is on the broader issue of how outsourcing is especially attractive in toxic policy areas where outsourcing delivery to commercial operators insulates the state from responsibility for decisions and, in the process, shifts blame to outsourcers.

Some of the most widely publicised scandals in outsourcing arise in this way – for instance, the brutal treatment of asylum seekers and the forced deportation of those who lose their appeals in the immigration control system. As in the case of the work capability assessments scheme examined below, fiasco is designed into a policy whose delivery is so brutal that it is bound to create uproar; outsourcing succeeds here because it finds a contractor to do the state's dirty work and outsources the political costs of the policy.

The series of outsourced contracts connected with work capability assessments (fitness for work assessments for disabled benefit claimants) is a classic example of designed fiasco. In March 2014 the Department of Work and Pensions and the outsourcing specialists Atos announced that the contract signed by Atos with the previous Labour government to carry out work capability assessments was to be cancelled a year early. Atos was to receive no compensation for the early termination of the contract, and while the public announcement of termination presented it as a mutual decision between contractors and contracted, it is plain that the company jumped before it could be pushed. The termination removed Atos from a contract whose delivery had become a byword for the farcical and the brutal, in decisions about when disabled claimants should be deemed capable of work. By the time Atos withdrew over 600,000 claimants had appealed against its decisions, and about 40% of the appeals had been upheld (Siddique 2014).

The origins of the whole scheme alert us to the fact that it was not just another attempt to outsource, but was specifically an attempt to outsource the retrenchment of the welfare state through invalidity benefit cuts which have been a policy objective for recent governments of all persuasions. Both the Labour government before 2010 and the Coalition that succeeded have sought to reduce the growing benefits bill accounted for by disabled claimants. The scale of this bill is illustrated by the size of the scheme (Employment Support Allowance (ESA)) designed to cope with benefit claimants. Thus:

The total caseload of new ESA claims received by the end of September 2013 was 3.5m; the total caseload for IB reassessments was 1.4m. The latest published statistics show that there were 2.46m ESA/IB claimants in November 2013. The monthly caseload of ESA new claims ranged between 65,000 and 75,000 in the year to September 2013.

(House of Commons Work and Pensions Select Committee 2014, p. 7)

The growing size of the disabled benefit population has been explained in competing ways: for some, large numbers on disability benefit reflect the willingness of government to park the long-term unemployed in this category, especially in areas where the old industrial economy has collapsed; for others, increasing numbers represent a growing recognition of disability as an obstacle to employment, so claimants are legitimately entitled to public financial support. But what is undoubtedly the case is that successive governments viewed the disability benefit bill as a problem, and the determination to control this bill increased after the great financial crisis of 2007–08 and the onset of a new age of public spending austerity.

Some of the problems faced by Atos (which was implementing a scheme introduced in 2008) had to do with its own incapacities, as it entered an area of work where it had no experience. But the primary source of difficulty was that any outsourcer holding this contract was obliged to impose (partly arbitrary) benefit restrictions on groups capable of mounting hugely politically damaging opposition. From the point of view of ministers the Atos contract not only outsourced the job of carrying out the assessments; it also tried to outsource the political damage. By the time Atos withdrew from the contract it had not only become a byword for corporate callousness in the campaign literature of those opposed to the policy; its staff were working in a toxic, and even dangerous, environment. As the Select Committee which conducted a post mortem on the scheme reported, a number of factors led Atos to seek an early exit:

the key ones were the *very toxic* environment in which their staff were being asked to work, including threats and security incidents, the lack of public understanding of the separate roles of Atos, DWP and tribunals in the process, leading to Atos being blamed for withdrawal or refusal of benefit; and the contract becoming less viable financially.

(House of Commons Work and Pensions Select Committee 2014, p. 29; our emphasis added)

What this account neglects is that the point of the contract was to assign to Atos the toxic task of implementation, and to allow ministers to assign blame to the outsourcer. The contract was designed to ensure that Atos shouldered the blame for the policy. As the Minister for Disabled People told the Work and Pensions Committee:

> when I arrived in the Department eight months ago, on my desk were an awful lot of letters from my colleagues – let us be perfectly honest about it – from across the House who had real concerns about how the assessments were being done and how Atos was performing ... it did become pretty obvious that Atos's confidence as to whether they could perform what we were asking them to do; our confidence; and the public's confidence was not sufficient, and so I did ask the team to negotiate with Atos as to whether or not Atos could leave the contract.
>
> (House of Commons Work and Pensions Committee 2014, Q447)

The politically toxic character of the scheme is well illustrated by the range of groups that lined up before the Select Committee to provide critical evidence against it, and about Atos's performance: they included the National Gulf Veterans and Families Association, Mind and Parkinson's UK. But the perceived political need to control the benefit bill, and the desire to outsource the politically toxic character of that task, continues to shape policy: in October 2014 the Department of Work and Pensions outsourced a successor contract to carry out the assessments to Maximus UK, the UK subsidiary of an international company with a wide portfolio of outsourcing contracts.

2.3 Routine cock-ups

Designed fiascos are important in themselves and because they challenge the view that fiascos are unintended failed outcomes produced as smart operators take advantage of a gullible state. But it should also be remembered that many fiascos are of a rather different kind which we call routine cock-ups. In our view, the endless series of routine cock-ups is not primarily the result of a Benthamite failure of government surveillance and control. The primary drivers of routine cock-up are the business models and behaviours of incompetent and irresponsible giant outsourcing companies, whether conglomerate or specialist. These issues are analysed in detail in Chapters 4 and 5 of this book. But in this section we want to make a point about how the existence of such incompetence among outsourcers undermines the managerialist rationale for separating delivery and execution.

This managerial ideology recognises two sets of actors – those responsible for policy strategy and those responsible for policy delivery – and assumes that each set possesses generic skills which can be promiscuously applied across numerous activities: on the strategic side, the skill to formulate the goals of policy and to write contracts that convert these goals into performance targets; on the delivery side, the capacity to mobilise transferable management controls and operating skills to ensure effective implementation. This assumption about transferable operating skills is challenged by the fiasco of the Atos work capability assessment contract. Atos – a firm with core competence and established reputation in IT delivery systems – could not convert these into the skills required to manage a policy initiative in another line of business which was more political than technical. The company lacked the specialised managerial skill, the tacit knowledge and the qualified personnel on the ground to have even a small chance of making the contract work without incurring huge public opposition about arbitrary decisions which were then not sustained on appeal.

Problems about non-transferable, sector-specific management skills are compounded by the business models of the giant outsourcing conglomerates. Our analysis in Chapter 4 shows how the stock market's requirement for growth has turned the outsourcing conglomerates into bidding machines boosted by acquisitions, which end up managing a sprawling portfolio of unrelated contracts. Here is the then chairman of Serco (one of the two big offenders in the 'tagging' scandal described below) summarising the range of contracts that his conglomerate manages:

> We focus on areas of justice and defence, transport and health services. Within justice, we run prisons, we do electronic tagging, we help with the Youth and Justice Board, we run immigration and detention centres. In defence, we run some army and air force bases. We do RAF Cranwell. We are a third share in the Atomic Weapons Establishment. On transport, we run docklands light railway and we are responsible for Boris bikes in London. In health, we work with a number of community and health care areas.
>
> (House of Commons Public Accounts Committee 2014c, Q5)

The key economic theme of Chapter 4 is that conglomerate growth through an ever larger portfolio of contracts produces the risk of financial crisis which undermines corporate stability and shareholder value. In this section we will make the related political point that the accumulation of contracts (almost regardless of the firms' technical competence or span of control) undermines service delivery and inevitably generates cock-ups. This explains why the giant outsourcing firms account for a disproportionate share of fiascos. In such cases, the firms will be publicly scapegoated for their failures, with the blame for fiasco being shifted on to their shoulders; nobody raises the question of whether the core executive is at fault for contracting with stock-market-quoted outsourcing conglomerates which are inherently unreliable deliverers.

Effective corporate management depends on internal controls within some kind of bureaucratic hierarchy. Firm-level control becomes hugely more difficult in a conglomerate managing a hastily assembled portfolio of complex business contracts from different sectors. The case of the tagging scandals that engulfed Serco and G4S in 2013 illustrates the problem. Audit showed that the Ministry of Justice was being charged, under contracts with the companies, for tagging offenders who were back in prison, had already had tags removed, had left the country, or who were even dead. The details and the consequences are not the concern here. What is critical is what the episode revealed about the absence of internal controls in the companies. The explanation given by the (new) chief executive of G4S for the failure, though self-serving, is entirely plausible: 'We did not have the systems in place that we needed to have ... Too much was left to a small number of individuals and we did not have appropriate checks and balances in place' (House of Commons Public Accounts Committee 2014c, Q116).

The difficulties of control are increased because the conglomerates are not only bidding for contracts to sustain organic growth, but also buying into contracts through the acquisition of smaller companies. When giant firms buy into contracts that they do not understand and have not negotiated, the result is 'we bought a pig in a poke' fiascos like the one relating to court interpreters. Capita acquired this contract shortly before it was due to come into effect when, in December 2011, it bought Applied Language Solutions (ALS). In October of that year ALS had signed a five-year contract with the Ministry of Justice to supply interpreters for court hearings. The agreement was a catastrophe from the start: ALS/Capita turned out only to be able to supply about a quarter of the interpreters needed; the contractors were obliged to use interpreters who had not been properly trained; cancellations and abandonments of hearings caused chaos in the courts; and when the Public Accounts Committee heard evidence in October 2012, nine months after the contract went live, the contractors still could not offer guarantees concerning the supply of properly trained interpreters. Even in 2014, when the National Audit Office revisited the contract, Capita was failing to meet its performance targets. The origins of the fiasco are straightforward: Capita bought ALS which was simply too small and inexperienced to manage the interpreting system; and the Ministry of Justice had culpably failed to explore ALS's competence and resources, or indeed to carry out any pilot of the project (NAO 2014 and House of Commons Public Accounts Committee 2012).

At this point, it is possible to sum up on designed fiascos and routine cock-ups. Each fiasco – such as failure to deliver on a contract to provide security for the Olympics, fraudulent billing, scandalous and incompetent management of capacity-to-work tests for the disabled – is met with increasingly insistent demands for more effective central control from the 'value for money' manager, the National Audit Office; groans of exasperation from the democratic overseers of the system, notably the Public Accounts Committee; and the almost endless scapegoating of those blamed for failure, whether executives in firms or public servants. But the origins of fiasco lie much deeper, in the fact that the system is being blindsided by the managerial ideology of separating policy and delivery which can be traced back to the *Next Steps* programme of the 1980s (Jenkins *et al.* 1988).

The system of outsourcing and fiasco sketched in the preceding sections is therefore not simply an unintended consequence of the conglomerate corporate form or of political guile in outsourcing politically toxic tasks. It is connected to a deeply entrenched ideology of public management which has ruled the minds of policy makers for a generation. It also shares the fate of that philosophy, in being subject to wildly contradictory pressures. It oscillates, depending on the political wind, between delegating control and centralising control. The contradictory history of the UK Border Agency is a perfect illustration: established in 2008 as a classic executive agency to contract out politically delicate tasks like border control and visa issues, it was reintegrated into the Home Office in 2013 following a protracted series of fiascos.

In this world, everybody is trapped: policy makers in the core executive, between philosophies that dictate contracting-out and the need to deal with the often politically explosive consequences of contracting-out; those responsible for negotiating outsourcing with commercial firms, between the pressure to put things on the market and the need to shape the markets; those responsible for post hoc scrutiny, like the NAO and the Select Committees, between the duty to identify failures and the need to exercise that duty within the policy constraints of the outsourcing system; commercial firms, between the imperative to chase contracts and the need to manage the costs of fulfilling those contracts, whether those costs are financial or politically toxic.

2.4 Takeaways for the concerned citizen

For the concerned citizen, this chapter offers one lesson above all: scapegoating and blame-shifting of the kind that dominates post mortems of fiascos is not enough. There is some incompetence, and some venality at the heart of the new economic constitution created by the rise of the outsourcing giants, but that is not the heart of the political problem. The heart of that problem lies in a delusionary ideology that makes a completely artificial separation between policy strategy and policy delivery; which assumes that delivery can only be competently done by commercial operators; and which, in giving these commercial giants the status of governing institutions, creates institutions that carry out public functions without effective public accountability. The theme of weak accountability recurs in later chapters of this book which show the limits of market discipline on outsourcing firms.

Chapter 3

Unjustifiable profit-taking on mundane contracts

Charge 2: Outsourcing contracts in sheltered mundane activities routinely cover profit-taking without risk at the expense of the taxpayer and workforce
The problem is (a) unjustifiable profit-taking in sheltered activities when limited capital investment is required and when market revenue risk is either absent or capped by provision for walk-away; and (b) cost reductions that improve margins are too often obtained by eroding wages and conditions which can undermine quality services, and save on wages in one outsourced activity at the price of increasing the social bill for wage subvention.

> Nowhere is there a clear, total figure for what we are paying and should be paying. The biggest issue is transparency, We have little idea of what is going on.
>
> (Councillor Clancy on the Service Birmingham outsourcing contract, quoted in Andrew White, *New Statesman*, 2013)

> We are committed to working in partnership with the council to reduce costs and improve services for the people of Birmingham.
>
> (Service Birmingham response to criticism by Councillor Clancy, quoted in Paul Dale, *Chamberlain Files*, 2013)

Only a small minority of outsourcing contracts become high-profile fiascos. The majority are quiet sources of revenue and profit for private contractors. Such contracts are routinely opaque, not only for citizens but also for elected representatives and public officials. The opening quote comes from a Birmingham councillor in 2013 complaining about the non-transparency of the outsourcing firm Capita's Service Birmingham contract for a bundle of services which, at its peak in 2011, was reputedly costing the council £120m per annum. The second quotation gives Service Birmingham's anodyne response to criticism, which simply repeats an unspecific promise to deliver better, cheaper services. Understandably, many citizens are therefore uneasy about whether and how the profit motive of outsourcers will undermine public service delivery; hence, the Labour Party proposals to cap profits at 5% on sales in National Health Service (NHS) outsourcing contracts (BBC 2015b). Economists have long argued that privatisation efficiency gains depend on general conditions like competition in the market or (by extension) effective competition *for* the market through competitive tender or franchising arrangements (Vickers and Yarrow 1991). Most mainstream policy makers retain the commitment (rhetorically, if not always in practice) to intensifying competition and view tackling market failures as the remedy for concerns about profiteering. Against this confusing background, our approach to mundane contracts is straightforward and pragmatic.

In this introduction, we start by explicitly defining three general legitimating conditions of profit in capitalist enterprise which, if satisfied, would economically and socially justify (a degree of) profit-making from outsourced service contracts. If these general conditions justify profit, they are not, of course, an adequate basis for organising the provision of complex services like health and adult care, which usually require planned investment and cross-subsidy that profit-seeking contractors could or would not wish to supply. But there is a more immediate, dire problem. In three successive sections of this chapter, we present case material which suggests that these general legitimating conditions are not met on many mundane contracts, which consequently represent unjustifiable profit-taking. This equates to capitalism failing on its own terms, with outsourcing contracts working as a device for privatising gains and socialising losses.

- *Condition (1) Profit is justified as a reward for risk taken after the contractor has invested capital and/or when future revenues are uncertain.* In section 3.1 we present illustrative examples which show these specific preconditions are not met because outsourced activities are typically labour-intensive with negligible capital expenditure, and often have predictable or state-guaranteed future revenues.
- *Condition (2) Profit is justified if competition for the market, through tendering or franchising, drives improvements in service delivery which cannot otherwise be obtained from services which are typically local monopolies.* In section 3.2 we draw on our research on rail to show that this condition is not met when bidders can game franchising systems and walk away so that, for example, train operating companies have an option on profits.

- *Condition (3) Profit is justified if the contractor can deliver effi-ciency gains and offer a higher quality and/or lower cost service.* The issues here are complicated, but in section 3.3 we show that cost savings in labour-intensive outsourced activities are often levered on cuts in workforce wages and conditions. Poverty-level wages make it difficult to recruit, train and retain a committed workforce; while the British state gains from the payment of lower wages in one account but loses from the increased demand for wage subvention in several other accounts.

3.1 Profit without risk

The specific terms and financial outcomes of most outsourcing con-tracts are unclear. The terms are usually protected by confidentiality clauses, and the financial outcomes obscured by the way in which profits from individual contracts are aggregated by a company which holds a portfolio of contracts. But in some cases, company accounts allow us to disaggregate and relate profits to specific activities and contracts. Below we analyse two examples. These contracts (like others we have seen) raise serious public interest issues about profit-taking without risk.

- G4S Forensic and Medical Services Ltd (G4S FMS) has, since 2005, assembled a collection of contracts with police forces and primary care trusts: the contracts variously include the supply of forensic medical services to the police; primary healthcare in prisons and immigration removal centres; and sexual assault referral centres. By 2010, G4S had agreements with 12 police authorities (PFM 2010). Turnover grew from £8.7m in 2008 to £15m in 2013 as contracts were added, with cumulative revenues reaching £73m by 2013. This is a relatively small operation for G4S, representing less than 1% of its UK business.
- Service Birmingham Ltd represents a new kind of municipal franchising system for big bundles of mundane services, which in Birmingham include IT systems for the council and for schools, call centres, council tax billing and payment services. A joint venture between Capita (two-thirds) and Birmingham City Council (one-third), the contract was originally signed in 2005 and covered the local authority call centre, IT (including for the City of Birmingham Library) and debt collection over ten years. It was expanded in 2011 to incorporate other services includ-ing council tax collection; and also extended for five years to

2020. While the total value of the contract was not disclosed, it was widely claimed that the cost was equivalent to 10% of the council's controllable budget; cumulative payments reached £1bn during 2013.

The forensic contracts extend G4S's role in core state functions of security and justice services. Despite some concern about private contractors running sexual assault referral centres (Travis 2013), these contracts have had a low profile. This was not so in Birmingham, where the (redacted) contract was finally published in 2014 after local campaigners had raised concerns about the absence of local accountability, the scale of the payments made to Capita and the penalties due if the council withdrew (Barnfield 2014). Concerns about quality of services (such as in the council's call centre) have led to changes. The ramping up of austerity has also significantly reduced the controllable budget so that the council has looked at Service Birmingham again, though the extent of reversal to in-house provision has so far been limited. The call centre was taken back in-house in 2014 with the transfer of 380 staff and expected savings of £42m over seven years (Elkes 2014). Press reports have suggested that the council is planning to terminate the entire contract early, though in 2014 the council rejected the option of immediate walkaway on cost grounds (Jee 2014).

The scale of the profits and returns on these contracts is summarised in exhibits 3.1 and 3.2. These graphs present two standard accounting measures of return.

- The return on sales (ROS), also referred to as the profit margin, is calculated as the profit divided by the sales revenue (in this case the annual contract value) and expressed as a percentage.
- The return on capital employed (ROCE) is calculated as the amount of profit divided by the total long-term capital invested (debt and equity) and expressed as a percentage.

The analysis discloses that the contracts offer solid if unspectacular returns on sales, which translate into starry returns on capital employed. Pre-tax returns on sales are 6.7% for Service Birmingham (2006–12) and 12.7% for G4S FMS (2008–13). In both cases, the main element in the cost base is labour; alongside this there are some extra requirements for the development of operating systems, for example IT systems in Birmingham. But because the requirement for capital investment is so small, the pre-tax return on capital is quite exceptional. In both cases, the ROCE is higher than in big

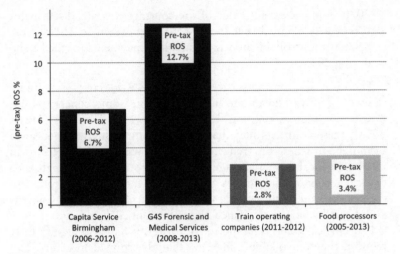

Exhibit 3.1 Pre-tax return on sales of outsourced activities, compared with food processors

Note: The food processors are Tulip and Dairy Crest

Source: Fame, Bureau van Dijk

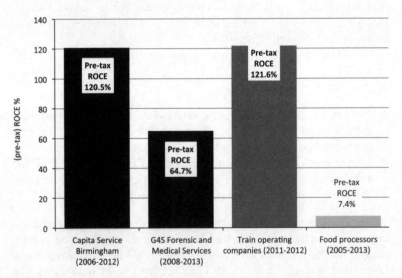

Exhibit 3.2 Pre-tax return on capital employed of outsourced activities, compared with food processors

Note 1: Capital is the summation of shareholder equity and long-term debt

Note 2: The food processors are Tulip and Dairy Crest

Source: Fame, Bureau van Dijk

pharmaceutical companies (where levels of return are protected by patents): G4S FMS produced an average of 64.7% over six years, while Service Birmingham achieved a striking 120.5% over seven years.

Exhibits 3.1 and 3.2 also include an average for the train operating companies, which enjoy similarly attractive average returns (and are discussed in the next section of this chapter). The high ROCE from contracts with such a low requirement for productive capital is a huge benefit for stock-market-quoted parent companies. As we shall see in Chapters 4 and 5, after periods of growth, such companies are ambitiously laden with financial capital (debt and equity) that has to be serviced – in a world where interest payments are obligatory and the stock market looks for return on equity (ROE) of at least 10%.

Two supplementary points suggest that the financial returns from these outsourcing contracts are easy money. First, there is little downside revenue risk in either case because the activity of forensic services offers growth, and because mundane municipal services are less exposed to downturns and cyclicality. There are many private-sector service activities with a low capital investment requirement where moderate returns on sales translate into generous returns on capital. But consultancy firms and commercial law partnerships, for example, operate in cyclical activities, where the risk is that revenue falls away so that labour costs are not covered. In Service Birmingham, analysis of the financial accounts shows that the revenue line is stable and predictable, while in G4S FMS, there is the opportunity to grow the business by adding new contracts so that turnover is up 50% in five years.

Second, the rates of profit and returns on capital obtained from outsourcing contracts for supplying services to the state are much higher than those obtained by suppliers to the private sector, which often have to make large productive investments in order to win contracts. This can be illustrated with supermarket suppliers, and exhibits 3.1 and 3.2 include average returns for two large food processors, Dairy Crest in dairy products and Tulip in pig meat. This benchmark comparison is interesting and relevant because in both cases we have a powerful monopsony purchaser – the local state in one case, the supermarket chain in the other. But the supermarket chains exert their power ruthlessly, while the local state featherbeds suppliers like G4S and Capita. The two food processors are among the top three in their market, with a portfolio of branded products, but both rely uncomfortably on supermarket own-brand contracts where margins are squeezed. While they have managed some uneven growth in revenues over the past decade, their return on sales average 3.4%. Because food processing requires capital equipment, the ROCE in these companies averages only 7.4%, considerably less than that on the outsourcing contracts or for train operators.

This is not an argument for the state to imitate the 'predatory contractualism' of supermarkets towards their suppliers (Bowman *et al.* 2013a). But the margins on many mundane outsourcing contracts appear over-generous and the local state routinely fails to safeguard citizens' interests. In this case we would add a qualification to the argument of Chapter 2 that ignorance does not explain the (central) state's problems with outsourcing. A local council may initially have purchasing power but will generally lack the knowledge to negotiate a fair contract. An outsourcing giant like Capita can acquire a series of contracts, learning from each case; it can also offset problems with one contract against another. However, a local authority like Birmingham City Council is a novice negotiator and can do little to deal with its mistakes, except try to find the cash to buy itself out of contracts.

This interpretation of local disadvantage is corroborated by the experience of Barnet in another joint venture with Capita. Barnet Borough Council in London has two ten-year contracts agreed in 2013: one contract covers back office support, corporate functions and customer services with an expected cost of £320m and saving of £126m; a second contract for development and regulatory services (including planning, highways, environmental health, trading standards and licensing) is worth £154m with expected savings of £39m (London Borough of Barnet 2013). Critics of these very large contracts allege that purported cost savings have not materialised. *ComputerWeekly.com* has reported that the majority of the £70m expected savings in back office functions will come from staff reductions, expected to cut the cost of service provision by 45%; however, because of the terms of the joint venture, Barnet Council will benefit only from an 18% reduction in service costs (Ballard 2012).

3.2 Franchise gaming and walk-away

Outsourcing extends the competitive tender systems traditionally used in government procurement of everything from army boots to paper clips. In the case of outsourced services, the bidders are typically competing for a franchise to deliver a service which will enjoy a local monopoly for the multi-year duration of the contract. It is therefore particularly important that the competitive bidding process restrains profiteering either by driving down the price the state pays for service or conversely (when the contractor accesses a revenue stream) pushing up the price the contractor pays for the franchise. Unfortunately, this does not always happen and the section below draws on our research into rail (Bowman *et al.* 2013b) to show how franchising is gamed by train operating companies so that they can avoid their promises to pay, instead walking away from contracts without significant direct penalty or long-term consequence.

Train operating in the UK is an attractive business for a small group of multinational transport and utility companies[1] which create special purpose vehicles (SPVs) to operate their franchises. Like many other outsourcing businesses, train operating requires very little capital investment, so that a modest return on sales turns into a starry ROCE. Across 17 existing franchises, the average profit margin (return on sales) was modestly around 3% in 2010/11 and 2011/12 (Association of Train Operating Companies 2013, p. 13; Bowman *et al.* 2013c, p. 15) and dividends, at about £160m in 2010/11, represented only 2% of passenger fare revenue (Bowman *et al.* 2013b, p. 29). But the train operating companies (TOCs) turned this 3% return on sales into over 120% ROCE in 2011/12 because they operate leased trains on track belonging to a separate infrastructure company, which since 2002 has been Network Rail (Bowman *et al.* 2013c, p. 15).

The possibility of profit for the TOCs is underwritten by the structure of the industry (which separates the operators from the capital-intensive infrastructure) and the forbearance of the state. If the 17 franchises and Network Rail were to be vertically integrated into one company, then the combined ROCE would drop to just 2%, which would not attract the likes of Stagecoach or Deutsche Bahn (Bowman *et al.* 2013c, p. 15). Further, capital expenditure and operations at Network Rail have been heavily supported by the state. For example, in the decade after 2002, capital expenditure was funded by the issue of more than £30bn of state-guaranteed bonds (Bowman *et al.* 2013b). The infrastructure company has not tried to recover these costs by levying substantially higher track access charges, and thus the TOCs are indirectly subsidised. In 2011/12, according to Department for Transport (DfT) data, 8 out of 17 active franchises were net recipients of direct subsidy, but this rises to 16 of 17 when factoring in this indirect Network Rail subsidy via low track access charges (DfT 2012a).

Franchises are usually allocated for periods of seven years or longer on the basis of the bidder's promises to pay the government from passenger revenue. More precisely, the government chooses between competing offers in terms of improvements to service, state subsidy required, and amounts paid to the state for the privilege in annual 'premium' payments. On attractive franchises, like the intercity main lines, the winner is the bidder offering the highest net present value (NPV) sum of premiums over the life of the franchise (on the basis of revenue and passenger projections). The DfT assesses bids to determine a suitable financial security (made up of bonds and other forms of guarantee) for the TOC to forfeit if the franchise is abandoned (DfT 2013); despite some reforms, these securities remain small in relation to the profit opportunities.

The successful bidder's problem is that rail operating is risky because (unlike other outsourcing business) premiums are paid out of a revenue line which is uncertain. And this uncertainty cannot be abolished because passenger numbers depend on changes in transport preferences and wider economic conditions including GDP growth. The DfT has mitigated but not abolished the risk with various schemes, including revenue support for TOCs should passenger numbers undershoot. And so the companies have learnt how to solve their problem by gaming the franchise system in a way which allows them to bid high and walk away from any franchise where things go wrong. First, they make 'back-loaded' premium payment offers, with most of the premium payments to be made in the later years of the franchise; second, if things do not work out, the franchise holder can walk away from the franchise in mid-term with modest direct penalties and no long-term consequences.[2]

Back-loading and walk-away with modest penalties comes in two forms which can be illustrated from the history of the East Coast main line under two successive franchises. The first is walk-away after banking considerable state-subsidised profits over many years, as with Great North Eastern Railways (GNER), a subsidiary of logistics company Sea Containers, which ran the East Coast main line franchise from privatisation in 1997 to 2007. The second is walk-away to stop early losses on a franchise, as with the National Express East Coast (NXEC) subsidiary of National Express, which took over the franchise in 2007 and walked away two years later.

'I would rather overbid and win than underbid and lose' said the chief executive of GNER and in 2005 that philosophy was applied to win a refranchising competition with an offer which was reportedly one-third larger than those of rival bidders and which was steeply back-loaded so premiums due in the final three years constituted over 50% of the total. From 2006 the parent company was in financial

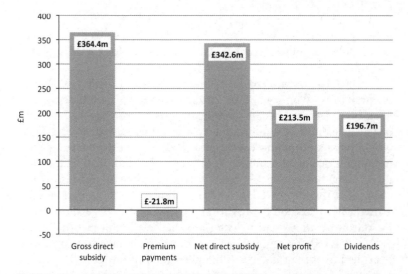

Exhibit 3.3 Great North Eastern Railways subsidy, premium payments, profit and dividends 1996–2007

Source: Company accounts, Great North Eastern Railways, various years

crisis and the franchise was in trouble (Milmo 2006). When GNER finally abandoned the franchise in 2007, the penalty for failure was losing £17m of shareholder equity, a £15m performance bond and £2.5m for re-franchising costs (McCartney and Stittle 2011, pp. 125–9). In context, over the decade 1996–2007 GNER had received £343m in net direct subsidy (after paying modest premiums) from which it found more than £200m of state-subsidised profit and distributed £197m in dividends to its parent, as illustrated in exhibit 3.3.

NXEC won an eight-year franchise in 2007 with another back-loaded offer so only 4% of premiums were due in the first two years, with 65% due in the final three years (Bowman *et al.* 2013b, p. 97). NXEC's bid assumed strong increases in passenger numbers, but the recession dragged revenues down and when the franchise was abandoned in 2009, National Express lost some £72m, comprising a £32m performance bond and a £40m subordinated loan (Peston 2009). No profits were made but losses were capped and commitments to premium payments of over £1bn were avoided.

In effect, risks on rail franchises are capped by the option to walk away with modest direct penalties. To make matters worse, there are no consequences for parent groups which break promises.

FirstGroup, for example, has been given back the Greater Western main line franchise, even though it had earlier walked away, and meanwhile had put in another back-loaded bid for the West Coast main line.

In 2007 the incumbent First Greater Western (FGW) subsidiary of FirstGroup won a new ten-year franchise with a bid combining back-loaded premiums and optimistic revenue projections. As illustrated in exhibit 3.4, according to the franchise agreement, FGW would pay no premiums for the first three years, before commencing premiums during the middle four, with the bulk due in the final three years, before which a break clause could be invoked (Bowman *et al..* 2013b, pp. 99–101). The bid predicted 8% annual revenue growth, but recession made this impossible and FGW walked away. FirstGroup paid a small penalty, reportedly £59.9m invested in the SPV, but avoided a reported £826m of premium payments promised over the life of the franchise (Plimmer and Wembridge 2011; Milmo 2011). There were subsequently no consequences for the way in which FirstGroup had abruptly stopped its losses on a franchise from which it had, since 2005, taken out £50 million of profits as dividends (Bowman *et al.,* 2013b, p. 59). Without any competitive tender, in October 2014 the government gave FirstGroup a direct award of the Great Western franchise for a further 3.5 years (Thomas 2014).

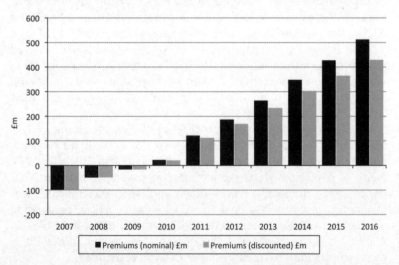

Exhibit 3.4 FirstGroup premium profile for winning the Greater Western franchise bid

Source: Company records, FirstGroup, various years

As FirstGroup had lost other franchise bids in 2014, the *Financial Times* reported analysts' views that these revenues would 'keep the company going nicely until 2019' (Lewin and Burgess 2014).

There is no sign that the DfT is learning from the way back-loading behaviours are repeated. Consider FirstGroup's 2012 bid for the West Coast main line, which failed after challenge by Virgin. The Transport Minister admitted 'completely unacceptable mistakes' in the DfT modelling used for the calculation of a £350m subordinated loan (Odell 2012). But civil servants and politicians never picked up on the repeated behaviour of FirstGroup, which had submitted yet another back-loaded bid, in this case making most of the £5.5bn NPV of premium payments optional (Bowman *et al.* 2013b, pp. 101–7). By way of contrast, market analysts understood that back-loading and walk-away were central to FirstGroup's 2012 bid for the West Coast main line. Assuming that for the first six years FirstGroup achieved its projected earnings before interest and tax (EBIT) of £305m, it would have far exceeded breakeven on its £255m initial investment, and could then abandon, avoiding onerous premiums due later on. As RBC Capital Markets argued:

> We still think the bid-in 10.4% revenues CAGR [compound annual growth rate] is aggressive, but the key is the non-linear premium payment profile. This affects the reward/risk tipping point in the contract. If profits go off-course early on, then maximum downside would be the walk away capital at risk. If the contract did deliver approx. £50m pa EBIT (so £38m post tax), then if FirstGroup walked away at any point after 6.8 years the operator would still be net up.
>
> (RBC Capital Markets 2012)

Why does the DfT not appear to learn from past experience about how TOCs game the system? In our view the problem is not government stupidity but co-dependence and the requirement to keep franchising going, which means that major players like FirstGroup are dominant and must be conciliated. Successful franchising requires an eager queue of bidders, which means low barriers to entry and exit, limited investment requirements which enable high returns, state subsidies to minimise risk and no consequences for broken promises.

3.3 Contracts levered on labour

Supporters of outsourcing argue that it delivers efficiency gains through providing a better and cheaper service. When labour can easily account for 80% or more of total costs in outsourced services (and the configuration of service delivery is fixed by contract and physical constraints), the practical emphasis is often on taking labour hours and cost out. In some cases, it is possible to reduce labour input, as Sodexo is doing with its ATM-style report-in machines for offenders, which will allow the firm to shed 30% of the staff in the newly privatised probation service (Travis 2015). However, the more usual outcome is cost reductions levered on labour through cuts in wage rates and conditions, such as pensions and holiday entitlement. Thus, contracts can work gradually to deliver profits through re-hiring new staff more cheaply when labour turns over. Employment in Service Birmingham Ltd has been rising as the scope of the contract expanded, while the average cost per employee (including indirect costs) fell to below £30,000 per annum by 2012. Overall, the proportion of the value added (the value of the output minus the value of bought-in goods and services) produced by the company accounted for by labour costs has fallen to less than 65%.

A more complicated cost structure with a requirement for fixed capital, as in residential care, brings little relief for labour if there is a financial engineering rationale for sub-dividing the activity into two businesses through property and operating companies. This effectively creates a new labour-cost-dominated operating business which can be pressured through higher rents charged by the property company.

There are exceptions where the workforce escapes the pressure for wage cuts: this is possible where the state offers financial support, or allows customers to be charged, or where work organisation can be configured to allow different conditions such as changes in hours or responsibilities. For example, in the case of rail (considered in section 3.2) state subsidy for train operators ensures that profits are levered on the state, limiting the direct pressure to reduce per head labour costs. Or services could be adjusted to reduce the number of workers required or to change their work patterns or entitlements, but without reducing wages.

More generally where such options do not exist, the logic of cost composition and wage reduction is well understood by outsourcing company management and politicians. In interviews with senior managers in financialised adult care operations, we were told that domiciliary care and residential care had been extensively outsourced by local authorities because private providers could do it more cheaply by paying lower wages. The same is obvious to civil servants and ministers when they evaluate outsourcing bids. We have had sight of a large outsourcing company's bid to take over a public prison: from the business plan spreadsheet of financials, it is quite clear that the private provider could only make the contract work financially by reducing the pay and conditions of prison officers.

The TUPE (Transfer of Undertakings and Protection of Employment Regulations) agreement protects the existing workforce against wage cuts after outsourcing but it does allow the hire of replacement workers on inferior pay and conditions. With the aim of curbing this practice, New Labour in 2003 introduced a code of practice covering local authority service contracts, but this code was rescinded in 2010 by the incoming Coalition government; this signalled that re-hiring on different (worse) terms was acceptable, and that such 'flexibility' was to be encouraged (Cabinet Office 2010). On this basis, outsourcing is a device that generally worsens pay and conditions, as explored below.

- In sectors where public and private providers work side by side, as in adult care or prisons, private providers pay less. The New Economics Foundation analysed Labour Force Survey data from 2011–14 on wages for residential care workers: the median wage is £9.45 per hour in the public sector, £8.50 in the voluntary sector and £7.23 in the private sector (Trade Union Congress and New Economics Foundation 2015, p. 92).
- The wage cuts are largest where outsourcing undermines the position of a strongly unionised, stable (and often male) workforce which has consolidated small bargaining gains over a period of many years. Thus in prisons the New Economics Foundation found a gap of more than £4 between the £14.18 median hourly rate of public-sector prison officers and the £9.98 earned by peers in the private sector (Trade Union Congress and New Economics Foundation 2015, p. 92).
- Where the outsourcer can systematically pay for less time than the worker actually puts in to the job, the bottom limit on outsourced wages is below the legal (adult) minimum, which in 2015 was £6.50 per hour. In domiciliary care, this is routinely done by not paying for travelling time, and by 'call cramming' which schedules tasks that cannot be completed within the standard time allotted for each visit. According to the Unison *Time to Care* survey, more than half of all care workers in 2011 were paid £6 to £8 per nominal hour, and many care workers must therefore be earning well below the legal minimum per actual hour (Unison 2011, p. 12).

But how and why does this matter? The most immediate empirical question here is whether wage cuts diminish service quality. The evidence is complicated because service quality is not easy to measure and outcomes are generally more mixed and complicated than can be publicly admitted by outsourcing companies or public-sector unions. The complexities can be illustrated by considering the two cases of prisons and adult care.

- *Paying workers more does not reliably produce higher quality services, because higher wages are no substitute for innovative service delivery, investment in facilities and effective unit management.* Like-for-like comparisons of prisons are complicated because of differences in groups of offenders and facilities and the multi-dimensional nature of performance. Private prisons are typically newer and larger than the often Victorian public-sector prisons; five of the ten largest prisons in the UK are privately managed (Trade Union Congress 2013, p. 12). The public-sector Prison Officers' Association claims that an academic study using matched pair comparisons between the sectors showed two public prisons to be 'generally superior' (Prison Officers Association 2011, pp. 16–17). But, as an early National Audit Office report (2003) pointed out, there are very large differences between best and worst prisons within both the public and private sector. Sturgess (2012) complicates matters by arguing that public prisons perform better on 'security measures' while private prisons perform better on 'relationship measures'. And the centrist Institute for Government think tank sums up agnostically that 'there has been no conclusive evidence to suggest that public and private prisons can be distinguished by key outputs' (Panchamia 2012, p. 4). The fundamental problem is that prisons of all kinds largely fail to deter crime or effectively rehabilitate offenders to prevent recidivism; they also tolerate internal cultures of bullying, drug abuse and self-harm. On this basis the important debate should be about different kinds of criminal justice systems.
- *Paying wages below living wage levels undermines the basis for delivering a good quality service, because the secondary effect of high labour turnover undermines the personal relation between carer and cared.* This is always damaging in care services where a high turnover workforce will not be adequately trained for complex tasks and cannot build relationships with service users. This is particularly relevant in adult care where sector managers accept that quality of care is strongly associated with low labour

turnover; indeed several financialised chains consequently use labour turnover rates at unit level as a key performance indicator in their operations. The problem then is that their lower wages tend generally to produce higher turnover. This point emerges very clearly from the New Economics Foundation study based on Labour Force Survey evidence: for residential care workers, median job tenure is 96 months in the public sector, 46 months in the voluntary, not-for-profit sector and just 29 months in the private sector (Trade Union Congress and New Economics Foundation 2015, p. 85). This effect is reinforced by differences in supervisory and management culture which many insiders believe is the single most important determinant of care quality at unit level; 38.9% of senior care workers in the public sector have degrees as distinct from 8.9% in the private sector.

All this is socially useful information for the citizen trying to make a judgement about outsourcing. But it is politically irrelevant when decisions about more (or less) outsourcing are not being taken after precise calculation of how low wages can go without undermining the basis of service quality, or after some exploration of how services could more imaginatively be improved by innovation and reinvention. Sector by sector, if the service can be done more cheaply after outsourcing, it can be outsourced without much regard for quality because that will get lost in measurement complexities or obscured by commercial confidentiality. If things go seriously wrong, then outsourcing has shifted blame so that it is the prison contractor or the domiciliary care chain which is to blame, not the policy itself.

The further problem is that narrow cost-saving calculations on one contract are a poor guide to the citizen's interest, because state savings on the wage bill after one activity is outsourced are counterbalanced by an increased bill for state top-up of low wages via the in-work benefits system. This requires us to understand what Keynes called the 'roundabout repercussions' of wage cuts. Keynes himself in the 1930s drew the distinction between benefits obtained by employers from wage cuts in one industry and the perverse effects on demand of general wage cuts imposed by all or most employers in a deflationary environment. This argument needs to be reworked for the very different context of the 2010s as the British struggle with the consequences of combining a flexibilised US-style labour market with European-style protections for the low waged.

Without anybody noticing, this combination of policies broke the connection between waged employment, independence and net

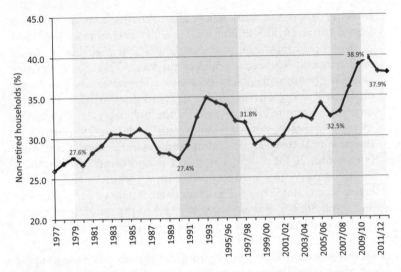

Exhibit 3.5 UK non-retired households receiving more in benefits than taxes paid

Note: Benefits include benefits in kind e.g. education and all taxes included

Source: 'The Effects of Taxes and Benefits on Household Income', ONS, various years

contribution to state finances which had been the cornerstone of the post-war settlement. Health and education services were always free at the point of use, means-tested housing benefit was available and some kind of family credit has been available since 1986. New Labour in 2003 introduced the Working Tax Credit and Child Tax Credit schemes under which HM Revenue and Customs pays out allowances which (after recent cutbacks) now cost £30bn per annum. On our calculations, summarised in exhibit 3.5, the proportion of *working* (non-retired) households receiving more in benefits than they paid in taxes increased from 27.6% to 38.9% between 1979 and 2010. Outsourcing which cuts wages only adds to this very British mess.

As we have argued, outsourcing in the UK has been driven and sustained by the private sector's ability to pay lower wages. But, since the 2015 election, that differential is being eroded as a matter of policy. Chancellor George Osborne is imposing austerity cuts which require the freezing of public sector wages and, at the same time, the Treasury is trying to curb the social cost of subventing private sector wages by a combination of cutting tax reliefs and mandating higher minimum wages. So, public sector wage rises are to be held to 1% per annum for another four years while the (private sector's) minimum wage is to be raised to £9 by 2020. Taken together, these policies will undoubtedly reduce the wage differential. The irony is that the narrowing or removal of this gap, which has provided the traditional rationale for outsourcing, will not lead to a return to public provision in the many cases where the public sector no longer has the financial resources and management capability to buy or build and operate facilities. Moreover, the private sector, which had counted on relatively straightforward labour cost reductions, will be left with a problem about how to make contracts work financially.

3.4 Takeaways for the concerned citizen

The first implication is that too little information is publicly available on the huge number of outsourcing contracts for mundane activities which do not end in fiascos. In the absence of systematic evidence, this chapter has argued from vignettes which are a cause for concern. They suggest outsourcing is a messy problem, not any kind of solution. The charges include: a lapse from capitalist standards insofar as outsourcing offers rewards without risk; a failure of political control when co-dependent state agencies cannot prevent major corporate players from gaming the system; and profits too often levered on labour through cuts in wages and conditions which serve no social purpose. Since 2008, most citizens have understood that banking and finance are sectors which work by privatising gains and socialising losses. Our analysis of routine outsourcing contracts suggests that this is part of a larger problem.

Notes

1 These predominantly fall into three categories: British PLC transport companies created following the deregulation of Britain's municipal bus services in the 1980s (FirstGroup, National Express, Stagecoach, Go-Ahead); subsidiaries of foreign state-owned rail companies (Arriva, Keolis, Abellio); and conglomerates which have focused on outsourcing and privatisation opportunities provided by the British state over the past thirty years (Virgin, Serco).
2 Penalties for walk-away have varied but have always been modest. In the most recent iteration of the franchise system, TOCs would have to supply a 'subordinated loan facility' alongside a 'performance bond' and 'season ticket bond', all of which would be lost in the event of a walk-away. The system is described in more detail in the original intercity West Coast main line franchise invitation to tender document (DfT 2012b).

Chapter 4
Undisciplined outsourcing conglomerates

Charge 3: Outsourcing has created giant conglomerates which are bidding machines focused on winning new contracts, turbo-charged through acquisitions
The stock market does not discipline but cheerleads for conglomerates whose growth is risky, because that requires entry into new sectors without operating competence or good judgement about what is achievable from the next bids and acquisitions. After financial crisis destroys shareholder value, corporate reset damages other stakeholders without ending the co-dependent relation between conglomerate and government.

2014 has been an extremely difficult year for Serco, and the magnitude of the provisions, impairments and other charges reflects the scale of the challenges we have had to face. However, there is a real sense that, having confessed our sins and in taking the punishment, we are now ready to start on the path to recovery.

(Rupert Soames, CEO of Serco, announcing the 2014 Annual Results (Serco 2015))

Serco has an extremely able and stable top management team. It has high visibility and a strong track record of organic profit growth. We estimate that 50% of growth is from new contract wins, and that only half those are 'large', which adds to the resilience of revenues. Management focuses on smaller, lower risk, less vulnerable contracts, which results in less order book risk. In an uncertain world we believe Serco's exceptional visibility, defensive revenues and growth track record warrant a premium rating which is not reflected in the current valuation.

(Brent and Shirley 2012b)

The opening quotation comes from Rupert Soames, the newly appointed chief executive officer (CEO) of the outsourcing conglomerate Serco, who looks back on a year of corporate financial

crisis, owns up to past mistakes and promises recovery led by a
management team. In 2014 Serco made a loss of £1.3bn, wiped
accumulated profits of £941m and required £555m of new equity to
shore up the balance sheet. After the company had issued four profit
warnings and lost 32% of its share price in one day, the City story of
2014 was that 'Serco is in a mess and only Rupert Soames can save
it' (Heath 2014). The second quotation comes from stock market
analysts writing less than two years previously about the old management team. The City story of 2012 was a very different one about
how the able and prudent senior management of Serco were delivering solid growth which was not yet priced into the shares, leading to
a 'buy' recommendation. The quotations open up several questions:
first, if outsourcing contracts offer high returns as argued in Chapter
3, why did a giant outsourcing company like Serco get into such dire
financial trouble; second, when the financial performance appeared
to change so radically within a couple of years, why did investors and
analysts not see the crisis coming and appreciate the risks of growth?

This chapter explores what went wrong for Serco before 2013
and, in a related way, for G4S, another giant outsourcing conglomerate which hit crisis in 2012. Section 1 of this chapter argues that
stock market pressure for growth turned these conglomerates into
bidding machines which delivered earnings by adding contracts to
their portfolio, and making debt-funded acquisitions. This was a
risky operational game of contract roulette, taking the conglomerates into unfamiliar activities where they lacked sectoral competence
and returns could easily be misjudged. Large conglomerates are
inherently opaque to outsiders and section 2 adds the point that the
risks of uncontrolled growth were poorly understood and largely
ignored by investors and analysts before their crises. In the growth
phase, the analysts acted as cheerleaders, encouraging management
imprudence, rather than exerting discipline; specifically, they ignored
the clear financial warning signs about how acquisitions were storing
up balance sheet problems. The final section considers how financial
crisis in 2013–14 led to corporate reset which promised an end to
pain for shareholders, inflicted collateral damage on other stakeholders and did not change the relation of co-dependence between
conglomerates and government.

4.1 Growth and contract roulette

This section is about growth: it analyses how analysts frame the
potential performance of outsourcing companies as growth stocks

and how corporate managements then deliver growth through a portfolio of contracts. Stock market analysts insist that outsourcing companies like Serco are (or should be) growth stocks, not income stocks like pipe and cable utilities. The difference is material because, on this basis, the outsourcing sector will have higher share valuations which anticipate future growth of earnings, rather than steady dividend payments. A smaller, slow-growing specialist company with an activity base in one or two sectors could offer steady returns, but it would not justify the growth narrative and associated share price.

Conglomerate growth in companies like Serco and G4S requires an expanding, constantly changing portfolio of contracts: thus management is playing a game of contract roulette where high returns from some contracts cover low returns and losses from misjudgements and mistakes. Outsourcing firms must continuously bid for new contracts to sustain revenue and most contracts have a relatively short, fixed life. Renewal is uncertain in a world where government commitment to creating competitive outsourcing markets means firms cannot be sure of winning any bid (even re-tenders). To deliver revenue growth, outsourcers must therefore add new and larger contracts, which often means bidding or buying into unfamiliar areas where senior management has no operating competence and contracts are often linked to policy reform, which provides a degree of novelty in the operating environment. Contracts can always be won by underbidding, which boosts revenue but not earnings. The task of the analyst or investor is then to read the signs of good growth using a series of operating indicators explained below: organic growth and the impact of acquisitions, (re-)bidding success, revenue visibility and margin defence. The related task of management is to deliver the numbers on revenue and earnings to justify a narrative about good growth with momentum.

Organic growth is widely seen as a key indicator, determined by the amount of new business available and success at winning bids. Analysts therefore pay great attention to government statements about their commitment to ever more outsourcing. For example, in 2012 J.P. Morgan's 'investment thesis' on Serco rested on a 'belief' that UK government outsourcing would continue to rise, while 'underpenetrated' international markets would grow (Plant *et al.* 2012b). Fiscal austerity is generally seen as positive in relation to business volume (McKenzie *et al.* 2014). While growth is an important indicator, stronger *margins* can offset slowing growth and are generally interpreted as a sign of management achievement (Cater and Woolf 2014).

Organic growth is preferred, but analysts also welcome *acquisitions* which promise to shift revenue upwards, buy in higher margins or build new areas of specialism. Deal-making has always been important: G4S is the product of the 2004 merger between the Danish Group 4 Falck and the UK's Securicor, and a slew of subsequent acquisitions have rooted it in a broad range of services and geographical markets. Green *et al.* (2007) approvingly noted that G4S preferred small, fast-growing bolt-on acquisitions that helped open more profitable, specialised parts of the security industry, such as electronic tagging and monitoring of offenders. This activity generated an estimated 4% of G4S's revenues and 7% of its profits, offering even better growth prospects than emerging markets (Saul 2007a). At this point, before financial crisis, most analysts cheered on acquisition-led growth. Credit Suisse said G4S was 'doing all the right things' (Green *et al.* 2007); others wondered whether G4S should borrow more aggressively to speed up acquisitions (Saul 2007b). The cheerleading continued after 2008 so that Serco's £385m purchase of Intelenet, an Indian outsourcing company, in 2011 (Serco 2011) was applauded by analysts (Brent and Shirley 2012a; Bamberry 2012).

The contract-based business model produces a 'volatile' share price (Magni *et al.* 2013a), even if acquisitions help smooth wins and losses. Companies must demonstrate 'contract momentum' (Bamberry 2012) and, as RBC analysts note, 'contract news flow remains a driver of momentum in the stock' (Brooke and Greenall 2013). The outsourcing conglomerates endeavour to make their game less like 'contract roulette' (Magni *et al.* 2013a) by building the bidding expertise and political capital necessary to win tenders and raise barriers to entry. All this covers a nervousness about how fortunes can change rapidly, so analysts are preoccupied by upcoming re-bids. HSBC in February 2013 noted that four imminent re-bids accounted for 12% of Serco's current revenues, and that the bidding process had become more competitive, meaning the winner would have to accept lower margins (Magni *et al.* 2013a). If the market demands contract wins there is clearly pressure to submit low bids, even if this creates later problems in delivering acceptable margins.

Uncertainty about winning contracts, however, is balanced by *visibility* (or certainty) of future revenues flowing from awarded contracts (Vanderpump *et al.* 2011). Discussing Serco in early 2014, Deutsche Bank noted: 'Typically the company has a fairly high degree of revenue visibility, given that the business is based largely on long-term contracts' (Chu and Sykes 2014). In 2012 J.P. Morgan went further in presenting Serco as a low-risk, recession-proof stock: 90% of its revenues were backed by contracts, which last an average of seven years; 90% of contracts were retained when re-bid (so annual revenue attrition is only 1.3%); 90% of revenues came from the public sector which was less volatile than the private; Serco supplied essential functions to the state which insulated the company from cuts; and Serco 'generally avoids revenue risk', as evidenced by its preference for 'the heavily subsidised Northern Rail franchise' rather than a riskier intercity franchise (Plant *et al.* 2012a).

What conglomerate management then had to do was deliver the growth of revenue and earnings which made these stories plausible. And this they did quite spectacularly as both G4S and Serco rode the rise of outsourcing as an economic activity. Exhibit 4.1 shows that from 1997 to 2013, Serco's revenues rose ten-fold, to nearly £5bn by 2012. Over the shorter 2004–11 period, G4S's revenues doubled, peaking at £7.4bn. Annual revenue increases are lumpy because growth comes from adding new contracts. Serco's annual growth rate ranges from 5% to 30%, with large gains usually achieved by acquisitions. Exhibit 4.2 shows the amount spent on acquisitions: this ranges from under £50m to over £300m per annum for Serco, while G4S spent over £50m in each year except 2013 and 2014, with a significant £400m in 2008. Acquisitions are opportunistic, and vary greatly in scale. In May 2008 G4S management boasted of having bought 'about 70-odd' companies in the preceding three years, and promised more (Thomson 2008). Of course, acquisition-led growth carries risks and after G4S's failed £5.2bn bid for ISS (Plimmer *et al.* 2011) and increased concerns about leverage, management developed a more conservative narrative about cost-cutting rather than deal-making, though as exhibit 4.2 shows, acquisitions did not halt entirely.

Bold bidding and acquisitions on this scale generated the Ponzi-style momentum enjoyed by many fast-growing quoted companies: success in winning bids and bolting on acquisitions brings in revenue and an extra lump of earnings which can be used to cover any problems about low margins and losses on existing contracts. It was never clear where exactly the profits came from when the companies were growing, although the relative profitability of different lines of business would become an issue if and when growth stopped. Exhibit 4.3 shows trends in operating profit margins:[1] Serco gradually built its margin towards 6% by 2012, before its crisis; similarly, G4S's operating margin peaked at 6% in 2009, before losing all the hard-won gains. As Chapter 3 showed, margins on favourable government

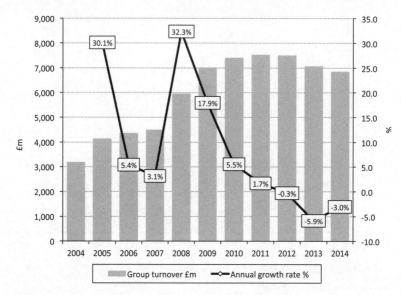

Exhibit 4.1a G4S group turnover and annual growth rate

Source: Fame, Bureau van Dijk

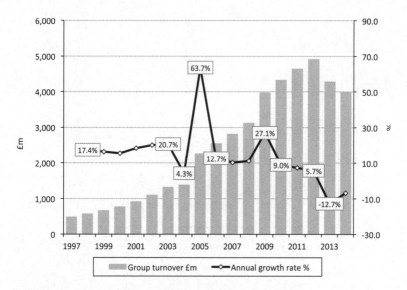

Exhibit 4.1b Serco group turnover and annual growth rate

Source: Company annual report and accounts, Serco, various years

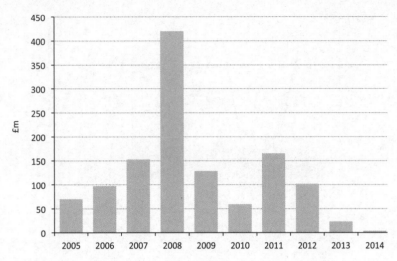

Exhibit 4.2a G4S cash spent on acquisitions

Source: Fame, Bureau van Dijk

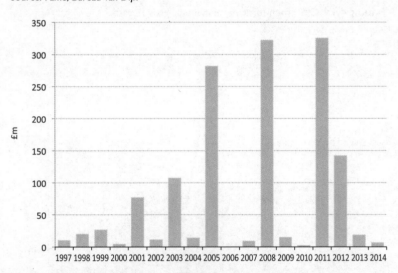

Exhibit 4.2b Serco cash spent on acquisitions

Source: Company annual report and accounts, Serco, various years

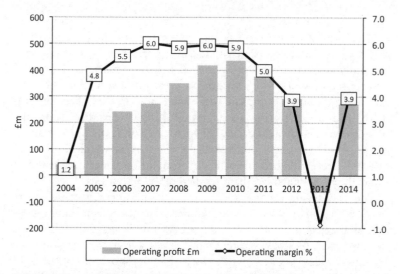

Exhibit 4.3a G4S operating profit and operating margins
Source: Fame, Bureau van Dijk

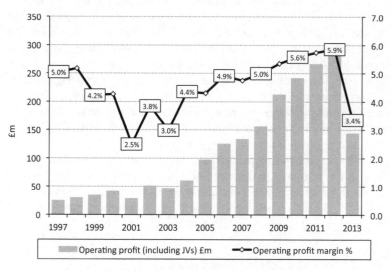

Exhibit 4.3b Serco operating profit and operating margins
Source: Company annual report and accounts, Serco, various years
Note: In 2014 Serco made a loss of £1,317m, representing a margin of −33%

contracts are often higher than 6%, suggesting such profits were routinely used to cross-subsidise low-return and loss-making contracts. Some analysts claim that UK government contracts have generally delivered, and are delivering, higher margins than most private-sector work, or government work elsewhere. For G4S, UK government contracts are said to provide 'among the richest margins in the group', delivering an estimated 12% of earnings from only 8% of revenues (Magni *et al.* 2013c; McKenzie *et al.* 2014; Plant *et al.* 2014). This point is confirmed by the way in which both Serco and G4S have clung to core UK government outsourcing businesses through crises which led them to shed other activities.

The end result was sprawling giant conglomerates which were black boxes, insofar as profit outcomes were dependent on unknowable changes in a mix of contracts whose individual profitability was not disclosed. As stock market analysts now admit, the conglomerate business model depends on holding a changing portfolio of the right contracts, accessing high-margin activities and exiting low-return activities, while delivering growth (Foteva and Chu 2014; Magni *et al.* 2013b); and doing all this on a grand scale. G4S is now the largest UK-listed contractor and the most international, operating across 125 countries to become one of the biggest employers in the FTSE 100. G4S's organisation into two businesses reflects its origins: around £1.3bn of 2013 revenues are for 'cash solutions', with a much larger £6.7bn coming from 'secure solutions', incorporating security contracts across a range of public- and private-sector clients (of which around £0.9bn covers welfare, care and justice services). G4S provides limited disclosure about the breakdown of specialisms in different regional markets, though 22% of total revenues come from the UK. Serco has been operating outsourcing contracts for around a century, originally in defence and later in transport, infrastructure and a range of public services: almost a quarter of its revenues come from UK central government, with a similar amount from local and regional government in the UK and the rest of Europe.

4.2 Opacity and balance sheet risk

Conglomerates classically trade at a discount because investors prefer to construct their own portfolios of shares in businesses with a core activity, and conglomerates respond defensively by denying they are like other conglomerates. Thus, G4S forestalled criticism of the conglomerate form by arguing that it strove for integrated services spanning sensitive and technically challenging tasks, which would lock-in long-term relationships (Sykes and Chu 2009; Saul 2007a). More importantly, they use segment reporting to make the mechanics of profit-making opaque so that the conglomerate becomes a 'trust me' story backed by aggregate numbers on revenue and earnings. All companies should disclose revenues, profits and assets according to meaningful business segments, defined (at company discretion) by business line or geographical market. But in a giant outsourcing conglomerate, the segment is typically a large aggregate which can conceal a multiplicity of problem contracts; and business segments can be redefined from one year to the next, making it difficult to obtain consistent and coherent time-series data on the UK public-sector business, or to judge the success of a major acquisition. Both Serco and G4S benefited from such constructed opacity and from the fact that stock market analysts ignored clear warning signs about interest charges and goodwill which could be read from their balance sheets.

The outsourcing conglomerates are large, complex companies: Serco typically has several hundred contracts at any one time,[2] while G4S had 879 subsidiaries in 2014. Analysts may glean or infer fragments, especially regarding larger contracts, but admit their understanding is limited and typically discuss only a handful, usually the largest contracts. Liberum notes that in 2011 Serco had only two contracts that produced more than 2% of overall revenues and that they had knowledge of just a few, meaning they could merely 'see the tip of the iceberg' (Shirley and Brent 2011). Canaccord analysts candidly state:

> The key risk in investing in the contracted revenue outsourcing businesses remains the difficulty in assessing the size, quality and timing of contracts. Outsourcers vary in the amount of detail they disclose about their pipeline of opportunities, often limiting commentary to little more than a discussion of the sectors in which their clients fall.
>
> (Cater *et al.* 2012, p. 6)

Such opacity was generally noted but not seen as a major cause for concern before the profits crisis. J.P. Morgan analsysts wondered aloud whether Serco's diversity might be a problem, but dismissed this with an assertion – no more – that diversity was a strength:

> There is a risk that Serco is a very diverse company and we sometimes question how it can be as good in all of its markets as some of its more focused competitors. That said, Serco's organic revenue growth has been better than its major competitors in recent years, which would suggest that it is

doing better. It may be that Serco's ability to transfer best practice between sectors gives it an edge, eg its experience of bids for welfare to work may help inform bids for the outsourcing of aspects of the probation service.

(Plant *et al.* 2012a, p. 28)

This kind of complacency explains why investment analysts did not anticipate the scale or timing of the crises at G4S and Serco; they were then surprised to find that the conglomerates were losing money on some of their major contracts, and that some acquisitions had gone wrong. The 2011 £385m Intelenet acquisition proved an expensive mistake and the disposal of that business was announced in Serco's 2014 strategy review. But, up to this point, the Intelenet business had vanished into a larger group segment and everything appeared to be working out: thus, 'Intelenet seems to have performed well, albeit it is difficult to track Serco's acquisitions once they have been absorbed into the group' (Brent and Shirley 2012a). This complacency was culpable because there were clear signs elsewhere of accumulating risk and trouble in the balance sheets of Serco and G4S. In a financialised company, when profit is being booked aggressively, the balance sheet assets either shrink (as with sale and lease back of property) or balloon as ever more assets are employed to deliver returns on equity (as with banks before 2007).

The warning signs in Serco and G4S were of inflating balance sheets. Most outsourcing contracts are labour-intensive, as noted in Chapter 3; and, as J.P. Morgan remarks, outsourcing companies prefer operating contracts, which do not require fixed capital investment (Plant *et al.* 2012a). The paradox then is that our two growing conglomerates had ballooning balance sheets of financial capital supporting operations with a negligible productive capital requirement. The main cause is that the acquisitions that bring growth have to be financed by issuing debt when cash flows are inadequate to cover the purchase price. This brings risk in two ways: first, debt has to be serviced from operating cash flow; and, second, deals put the difference between the purchase price and the balance sheet value of the assets acquired into the balance sheet as goodwill, which will be written down against profit if the acquisition does not deliver.

In the case of G4S, total debt (long- and short-term) rose towards £2.5bn by 2012, as the company expanded its footprint. Although debt declined modestly in 2009, net debt[3] levels increased relative to (falling) earnings to a ratio of 3.8 in 2012, and more than 70% of the capital employed. Since then, G4S has focused on reducing this ratio towards a more conservative level of 2.0 through raising equity and selling subsidiaries, allowing debt to be paid down. This is defensive restructuring and analysts expect a return to bolt-on acquisition once the balance sheet is strengthened (Chu *et al.* 2013; Greenall and Brooke 2013). Serco also became more leveraged, with debt generally between £0.7bn and £0.9bn after 2008, and the debt to earnings ratio deteriorating as earnings collapsed in 2013. A heavily capitalised G4S struggles to reach a 10% return on capital employed (ROCE), with return on equity (ROE) around 15%. Serco's returns are stronger with 12–15% ROCE and 20–35% ROE but with both measures declining substantially since 2010.[4]

The cash cost of servicing new debt is not the only balance sheet problem arising from growth through acquisition; the increasing amounts of goodwill capitalised in the balance sheet makes profit increasingly vulnerable to impairment charges. Exhibit 4.4 shows how goodwill grows disproportionately from a level equivalent to around twice the value of tangible fixed assets (i.e. land, buildings, equipment and vehicles) to more than seven times for Serco in 2013. Although G4S was more leveraged than Serco, its accumulated goodwill is more modest in relation to tangible fixed assets, reaching a peak of four times. Problems can arise because companies are required to review their capitalised goodwill; if it is considered that the ability of these assets to generate future earnings deteriorates, the value of goodwill must be written-down in an impairment charge against profits. Such impairment contributed to the collapse of Serco's earnings in 2014 when write-downs exceeding £1bn were recorded. Such write-downs included not only goodwill charges but bidding costs and systems development expenditures which previously had been capitalised, with the effect of enhancing profits and returns. Few analysts had noted the capitalisation of such costs, though this practice should have been read as a warning that Serco was a struggling company concerned to present itself in a favourable light.

Hindsight is a wonderful thing. The analysts (who had not changed their story to reflect clear warning signs before the crisis) were wise after the event and then began to openly question the quality of earnings during the previous decade. After the crisis, UBS described Serco as 'a business that has not grown profit [excluding the Australian immigration contracts] since 2009' (Cater and Woolf 2014). The average margin of 6% from 2009–13 'was flattered both by some high margin contracts and aggressive accounting judgements', and the 'balance sheet was weaker than it looked' (Cater and Woolf 2014). For G4S, Deutsche Bank estimated that all the £160m increase in profit (before interest, tax and amortisation) from

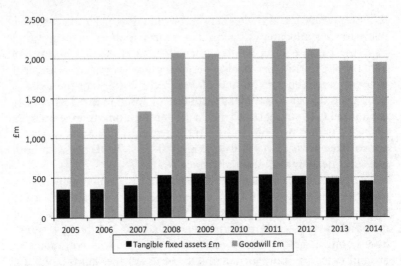

Exhibit 4.4a G4S tangible fixed assets compared to goodwill
Source: Fame, Bureau van Dijk

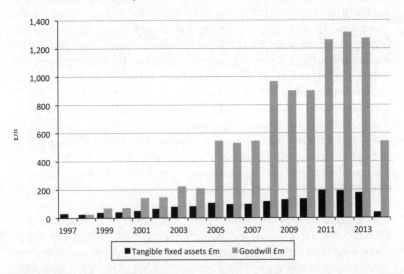

Exhibit 4.4b Serco tangible fixed assets compared to goodwill
Source: Company annual report and accounts, Serco, various years

2005–13 came from acquisitions (Foteva and Chu 2014). Moreover, G4S's margins were only sustained around 7% because of business disposals and acquisitions (Magni *et al.* 2014).

Analysts have thus responded to conglomerate crisis by becoming immediately more cautious about the performance and trajectory of the outsourcing conglomerates. They now agree that the conglomerates face a more difficult operating environment and should expect lower margins on contracts which transfer more risk to outsourcers as central government becomes more financially astute. RBC's analysis of outsourcing companies now overlaps with that of radical critics of outsourcing: 'from a political standpoint we struggle to see why the outsourcers should make ROIC's [return on invested capital] of 20% plus at the expense of the taxpayer' (Brooke and Greenall 2013). If this represents a degree of wisdom, there is no reason to believe that outsourcing conglomerates are any less opaque or that analysts will now make better judgements of accumulating risks and future performance. Indeed, by the end of 2014, Serco and G4S had completed a corporate reset and the consensus was that the worst was over for the two conglomerates.

4.3 Corporate reset and ongoing co-dependence

Corporate reset is a stereotyped manoeuvre which resolves company crisis and avoids fundamental business reform; the corporate vehicle crashes, a new management team is brought in to 'kitchen sink' provisions against profits in one annus horribilis; the new team admits the mistakes of the old management team and promises a more prudent approach; the new team promises that it will now deliver shareholder value but makes no fundamental change in the business model. Reset is absolutely necessary when, as in banking after 2008, the issue is a lack of probity and control as much as unprofitability. So it was in G4S from 2012 and Serco from 2013, where profits crisis was compounded by scandalous failure. For example, G4S failed to deliver security for the London Olympics (Reuters 2014; Booth and Hopkins 2012) and faced questions about the death in custody of deportee Jimmy Mubenga (BBC 2014); both companies held electronic offender tagging contracts which became an acute embarrassment because the allegations here were about possible fraud as much as incompetence (Plimmer 2013b). This required more than the usual Public Accounts Committee grilling of a CEO, with government insisting that both companies undergo 'corporate renewal' to demonstrate fitness for new contract awards (Warrell 2013).

Serco's problems mounted through 2014, with four profit warnings in the course of a year and more senior resignations, as the exit of Serco's chairman, Alistair Lyons (Plimmer 2014), was followed by that of the chief financial officer, Andrew Jenner (Robinson 2014). In

'Onerous contract provisions' (including £115m for COMPASS; £66m for Royal Naval Fleet Support)	£456.7m
Asset impairments and other provisions	£288.6m
Goodwill impairment	£466m
Other exceptional costs	£195.5m
Total write-downs, Serco 2014 results	£1.6bn

Exhibit 4.5 Serco's crisis and the 2014 write-downs

Note 1: COMPASS is the UK asylum seekers' housing contract

Note 2: An 'onerous contract' is one that is expected to be loss- making; the provisions recognise those expected future losses.

Source: Company annual report and accounts, Serco, 2014

November 2014 the company updated its strategy review, disclosing £1.5bn of 'balance sheet adjustments' (Serco 2014), later restated as £1.6bn in the full year results (Serco 2015), as summarised in exhibit 4.5. Among goodwill and other write-downs, particularly striking was the admission of significant contract losses and future provisions, totalling around £200m, on UK public-sector contracts. This included a £115m expected shortfall on COMPASS, the contract to house asylum seekers, where Rupert Soames has explained that the company is 'suffering shockingly large losses', with unexpected volume increases exacerbating the problem (Plimmer 2015a). Analysts noted the 'sheer scale' of the adjustments required to stabilise the company (Brooke 2014; Cater and Woolf 2014).

G4S's crisis became evident earlier, leading to a net loss of £342m for 2013. The resignation of CEO Nick Buckles came in the wake of the 2012 Olympics security scandal (which incurred an £88m contract loss) and the failed 2011 bid for Danish company ISS, which cost £55m (Hill and Plimmer 2013). The fiascos were reputationally damaging and commanded media attention, but at G4S, as at Serco, they were only a small part of a larger financial crisis: G4S's settlement over electronic tagging overcharging with the Ministry of Justice in 2014 represented just 4% of the overall contract value (£136m). The major financial problems concerned the need to clean up the balance sheet, where accumulated problems had to be dealt with through share issue, business disposals and a downscaling of acquisition spending.

The main symbolic element in reset was the replacement of the CEO: at G4S in 2013 Ashley Almanza replaced Nick Buckles, and at Serco in 2014 Rupert Soames replaced Christopher Hyman. Rapid turnaround was impossible because problems were deep-seated, but new management was ostentatiously contrite about the mistakes of the previous regime. Serco presented its review process as onerous, turning over 'stones' to identify problem contracts. And the new CEO was frank about two 'strategic mis-steps'.

> First, confronted by slowing growth rates and increased competition in its core markets, and wishing to maintain its historic levels of growth, the Group diversified its portfolio significantly, sometimes by acquisition, and often into areas that required very different skills. In so doing, Serco lost some of its focus and diluted its operational expertise. Second, it has concentrated too much on winning new business and has failed to manage effectively the fact that over recent years there have been significant advances in public sector contracting, particularly in the UK, with new models that transfer substantially more risk to suppliers. As a consequence, we now have a number of contracts which are making large losses, and others which are in sectors where we are sub-scale.
>
> (Serco 2014, p. 4)

Similarly, Ashley Almanza, the new CEO of G4S, admitted errors of 'overreach' (Thomson Reuters 2013, p. 25) and, like Soames, promised a more conservative approach to winning new business. Through this self-criticism, the new CEOs admitted that their outsourcing conglomerates had (earlier) escaped management control and made repeated misjudgements regarding their ability to (profitably) fulfil contracts and manage a complex portfolio.

All this supports our charge that management was not in control of these outsourcing conglomerates in their growth phase; and it is hard to believe new management promises that the future will be different from the past when the conglomerate business model and the stock market's expectations have not changed at all. Corporate reset is not the same as recovery or turnaround, but it usually ends the pain for shareholders who can expect some short-run bounce in the share price. At the same time, reset usually involves collateral damage for other stakeholders. When boom turned to bust, the conglomerates acknowledged that they had under-priced some contracts in the past (Plimmer 2015a), whether deliberately to win business or inadvertently because they did not grasp the requirements. In reset mode, the conglomerates will withdraw from unprofitable contracts and improve margins by squeezing labour on their other contracts.

- Serco and G4S have both been shuffling their portfolios of contracts (Thomson Reuters 2014), retreating from contracts or areas of business that do not deliver sufficient margins and adopting a more selective approach to future contracting. For example, G4S put its US Government Solutions business up for sale (G4S 2014) while Serco has announced that it does not intend to bid for further contracts in UK healthcare (*Health Services Journal* 2014). The end result is the conglomerate as a bidder which tries to cherry-pick the most attractive outsourcing contracts and may attempt to exit as quickly as possible when contracts become problematic.

- Serco and G4S have both been trying to reduce costs and thereby improve margins across the board. In G4S's new approach, acquisitions are expected to be less important, with more emphasis on wringing profitability from existing contracts (Thomson Reuters 2014). Inevitably, this means squeezing the workforce. In G4S's case, wages take 90% of the value added[5] produced even in good times, so small labour savings translate into large shareholder gains (Cater and Brown 2013; Foteva and Chu 2014; Magni *et al.* 2013d). As we argued in Chapter 3, pressure on already low wages and conditions is likely to undermine the basis for high-quality service delivery.

The corporate-level pressures for cost reduction are intensified by continuing austerity and public-sector spending cuts, together with criticism of overly generous outsourcing contracts by the Public Accounts Committee. Liberum analysts noted that in some areas contractors had become used to 'supernormal profits' which have been subject to increasing crackdown (Brent and Shirley 2013, p. 6). Pressure seems particularly acute on re-tendered contracts (Plant *et al.* 2012a) and, if the government has been relaxed about the absolute level of profitability of contractors, it is concerned to find contract savings. In 2010 the Cabinet Office required members of its major suppliers group to sign a Memorandum of Understanding setting out new terms for existing contracts, and contractors were expected to make an £800m contribution to the government's £81bn cost-saving programme. The very British response of conglomerate management has been to pass the punishment down the line to their suppliers. Serco was embarrassed when a letter subsequently sent to its main suppliers asking for a 2.5% rebate on costs was published and had to be retracted (Plant *et al.* 2012a); and the Cabinet Office was more recently asked to investigate pressure by another conglomerate, Capita, on its small sub-contractors involved in central government contracts (Green and Wright 2015).

All these conglomerate adjustments further undermine their claims to usefulness and excellence. An opportunist conglomerate holding a shifting portfolio of contracts is not a stable provider institution that can build and transfer expertise; nor can it easily learn, improve and encourage social innovation. Conglomerate management draws on a set of generic skills, and sector-specific expertise may become less valued than ability and willingness to manage costs. While government picks up the pieces after corporate retreat, it cannot step back in and resume public service because the public sector will have lost the kinds of institutional knowledge and expertise that previously existed in the public service organisations. Where outsourcing conglomerates are involved, the most important general result of outsourcing is not better or worse service delivery but a relation of unstable and destructive co-dependence between government and conglomerate. G4S and Serco continue to see public-sector outsourcing as their core business, while the state favours large corporate bidders (including conglomerates) in a way that stores up problems.

4.4 Takeaways for the concerned citizen

Outsourcing is not just about allocating contracts, as much of the existing literature supposes, it is also about creating companies, both the giant conglomerates considered in this chapter and the sector specialists considered in the next. In the case of the conglomerate, the individual contract is incorporated into complex, uncontrolled and unstable companies holding large portfolios of contracts where the sources of profit and the nature of cross-subsidies are invisible. This produces all kinds of secondary risks which are not registered in the literature on outsourcing. We would not argue that all conglomerate outsourcers will necessarily descend into crisis, but their growth is always high risk, and our analysis of Serco and G4S raises questions about the fundamental premise of outsourcing, that the private sector can do it better. How can the private sector do it better if, as this chapter argues, outsourcing is led by conglomerates which lack distinctive sectoral competences and are valued by a stock market which is unable to monitor and discipline their imprudence? Much faith is placed in the disciplinary judgements of capital markets which are expected to backstop the misjudgements of government and other actors. Instead this chapter shows how stock market judgements on companies which hold portfolios of outsourcing contracts only add complications. Worryingly, the stock market has gained no transferable knowledge from its pre-2008 misjudgements of banks and banking, so that it remains much too trusting about what is going on inside black box firms as long as their growth delivers pleasant surprises.

Notes

1 The operating profit margin is the operating profit divided by the sales revenue and is expressed as a percentage. Operating profit is profit before interest and non-operating items (i.e. costs or revenues that do not result from normal ongoing operations, such as the gain or loss on the sale of an asset). The profit margin is also sometimes referred to as the return on sales (ROS).
2 According to analysts at RBC Capital Markets 'the group is made up of 800 disparate contracts run like individual companies' (Brooke and Greenall 2013).
3 Net debt is equal to short- and long-term debt, minus cash and cash equivalents.
4 These rates of return are based on post-tax profits.
5 Value added is the difference between the value of the output (sales revenues) and the cost of the bought-in goods and services used to produce them. The value added is then applied to internal labour costs, depreciation and other charges.

Chapter 5

Outsourcing specialists and the gaming of limited liability

Charge 4: Outsourcing which brings specialist expertise also exposes essential service delivery to financialised practices
Within these practices the use of inter-company loans and special dividends secure private gains at social cost because they create fragile subsidiary companies. These practices involve a 'gaming' of limited liability privileges which breach the implicit contract between investors and the state which grants such privileges.

The business was ... (demerged from) water company Severn Trent ... in 2006 and then taken private in a 2008 leveraged buy-out by private equity groups Global Infrastructure Partners and Montagu Private Equity. The high leverage in that deal caused the company to get into trouble during the recession, and in 2013 hedge funds Angelo Gordon & Co, Avenue Capital Group and Sankaty Advisors took over ownership.

About half of Biffa's revenues comes from its industrial and commercial division, where it serves customers including supermarkets group Sainsbury's, the Royal Mail and Pret a Manger, and is the largest collector of rubbish and recyclables from businesses in the UK ... In domestic waste collections, Biffa is second to Veolia ... Across the UK, Biffa operates 19 material recycling sites, three anaerobic digestion plants, seven refuse-derived fuel facilities, six chemical treatment works and a plastics processing factory.

(Cave 2015)

These two quotations are taken from a *Telegraph* profile of the waste management company Biffa and help to explain why the problems of outsourcing cannot be solved by rejecting conglomerates and preferring 'sector specialists' who operate in one or maybe two areas of the foundational economy. Biffa is a large specialist outsourcer with UK turnover of more than £800m; depending on measure and market, Biffa is number one or two to the British waste subsidiaries of French parents, Veolia and Suez Environmental. But Biffa is also a case study in financial engineering because this mundane business has had four ownership changes in ten years as successive owners aimed to cash out gains and/or stop losses. After a leveraged buyout by private equity collapsed in 2013, Biffa passed into the ownership of hedge funds which will in due course exit by selling to private equity, or to a trade buyer if they cannot float Biffa as a public company. The order of the quotations is also significant because, in successive paragraphs of the profile, the *Telegraph* first discusses ownership changes which impact profitability before turning to the mundane ongoing activity that generates the cash.

In this chapter we find specialist outsourcing firms with the same order of priorities because, just like the conglomerates in Chapter 4, their strategies are informed by financialised calculations where accounting and law expertise is as important as their operating competences. Classically, the result is some form of tiered corporate structure where the superordinate aim is to immure profit within the corporate network so as to restrict the claims of the state and other stakeholders. Within such structures, investor parents can gain from a variety of moves, including the opportunist use of inter-company loans and special dividends to extract cash and depress taxable profits in the subsidiary; or, alternatively, investors can load subsidiaries with debt which makes them financially fragile and prone to sudden collapse.

In this chapter, the Veolia case illustrates the first strategy. The revaluation of assets as a consequence of a new accounting rule provided an opportunity to hollow out the UK subsidiary through group loans and special dividend payments. This channelled cash up the corporate chain to the French parent but left behind a more fragile UK subsidiary that now pays considerably less tax to the UK government. The second case, Biffa, shows how fragile subsidiaries can be created by 'load the donkey/flog the donkey' strategies that over-capitalise subsidiaries with debt so as to save tax and improve equity returns. This went spectacularly wrong because interest payments restricted investment in vital new recycling plants and the financial operating model could not cope with a downturn when industrial waste volumes declined. The Biffa subsidiary was insolvent after a one-off goodwill impairment charge and the resulting mess imposed substantial losses on multiple stakeholders and left an enduring legacy of under-investment in service infrastructure.

These outcomes are directly a material, social and economic problem. But the use of tiered corporate structures also games limited liability and thus breaches the spirit of reciprocity between the private investor and government which is the basis for granting the privilege. This chapter therefore begins with a brief account of the history of limited liability, the original arguments about its conditions of use and its appropriate field of application. In the case of specialist outsourcers we see how limited liability has become detached from those original – and worthy – intentions.

5.1 The uses and abuses of limited liability

In its millennium edition *The Economist* (1999) presented limited liability and equity investment as a crucial nineteenth-century institutional innovation which was subsequently 'the key to industrial capitalism'. This innovation has a different history in various industrialising countries and in this section we review the British history of granting limited liability as a privilege in the 1800s before turning to argue about how the privilege is being abused in the financialised capitalism of the 2000s.

Limited liability is a privilege for the investor but potentially a moral hazard for society because it allows the investor to make unlimited gains from a company's activities while capping downside losses; an investor can lose their equity stake but is not otherwise responsible for the company's outstanding debts. In the seventeenth century limited liability privileges were granted by the Crown to only a select group of joint stock firms like the East India Company. These privileges were gradually generalised to all private firms through a series of amendments to the Companies Acts between 1844 and 1862, most notably the 1844 Joint Stock Companies Act and the 1855 Limited Liability Act. There is some debate as to whether these acts were passed because of mounting technological pressures or the growing political power of a rentier class (Ireland 2010); but the laws were publicly defended with arguments about economic efficiency, not the rights of shareholders as owners (Ireland 2001).

From the 1840s onwards, limited liability was presented as a necessary concession if the UK was to enrol investors in large infrastructure projects which would augment social overhead capital. This argument was developed for railways, pipe and cable utilities, iron making, mining and shipping, the sectors which accounted for a large part of what was quoted on the London Stock Exchange by the 1880s (Lee 1986, pp. 54–5). Several interrelated arguments were made in support of limited liability. First, it was argued that passive investment by small rentiers would be encouraged by sheltering investors from corporate debts; second, equity investment would be particularly valuable in the case of large-scale, long-gestation capital-intensive projects where low risk was in itself not enough to attract private investors; third, society would benefit from an increase of the national economy's capital stock, which was the superordinate aim of the two main British acts. Limited liability therefore came with a clear idea about economic benefits as well as expectations about mutual/reciprocal relations between the state and investors.

Nineteenth-century limited liability was thus grounded on a general principle of reciprocity, whereby government granted loss-limits for investors on the understanding that they would put something back by helping to build the nation's infrastructure for the benefit of the social weal. There never was a golden age of corporate social responsibility when railway magnates like George Hudson immediately rediscovered company promotion (not operation) as a source of gain (Reed 2004). But irresponsibility was limited by the framing of the Company Act reforms of 1844–62, which envisaged limited liability as a special case primarily relevant to capital-intensive, social-overhead projects. It was only through historical accident, most importantly the 1897 Salomon vs Salomon verdict, that limited liability was extended to corporate owners and their subsidiaries, so that (in any activity) it became possible to tier subsidiaries upon subsidiaries, with each holding the privileges of a separate legal person (Blumberg 1986, p. 608). This outcome may have followed English law's precedent-based process faithfully, but it came at a price because the combination of limited liability with complex group structures certainly facilitated irresponsibility (Blankenburg *et al.* 2010; Toporowski 2010).

Nevertheless, parent–subsidiary tiering was used in a moderately responsible productionist way by British and American giant firms for most of the twentieth century. If we consider giant auto companies, their major subsidiaries were typically organised by territory for different national markets or by product lines like truck or car; there was then typically a second functional tiering within territories between assembly, finance and parts. This allowed the parent considerable latitude about where profit was taken because transfer pricing between subsidiaries allowed profits to be moved between jurisdictions and activities. But, beyond that, irresponsibility was limited because it was generally supposed that the parent would have a benign and supportive relation with major subsidiaries. In the stylised history of US giant firms by Chandler (1962), the role of the parent in the 'multidivisional firm' was to formulate strategy and allocate capital among subsidiaries competing to improve performance above a hurdle rate. Predation did happen, but only exceptionally, as in the case of Daf trucks and its Leyland subsidiary in the early 1990s, when the parent was financially distressed and desperate (Adcroft *et al.* 1993).

The general relation of parent and subsidiary is completely different after financialisation, when the parent is directly a fund investor with an exit strategy like private equity or hedge funds; or when the parent is a public company under fund or family pressure to deliver shareholder value. This creates a series of problems about predatory or opportunist parent companies where tiering can be used to game limited liability. These problems are aggravated by activity characteristics when privatisation and outsourcing allow fund investors and corporates to move into foundational activities like utility services or health and welfare. In the next few paragraphs we will briefly describe these general problems which are then illustrated in the following two sections by the Veolia and Biffa cases.

This financialised relation between parent and subsidiary is predatory when the parent pulls forward income and strips out the subsidiary's shareholder funds. This can be done through practices such as the payment of special dividends from the subsidiary or lending at high rates to the subsidiary, even if it means putting the subsidiary firm at risk. That risk is something an outsourcing subsidiary has to bear if it means a determined parent company can get their money out quickly. This process of de-temporalising returns is often disruptive for others because it imposes social costs for private gain. Bringing returns forward will either come at the expense of another claim on income such as the state's claim for tax revenues, or at the cost of reduced service benefits for households, when investment is starved and service upgrades are delayed due to increased interest payments.

The problems are aggravated in foundational economy activities like waste because continuous service has to be delivered in essential services, even if a corporate subsidiary becomes financially distressed or insolvent. Socially essential foundational activities cannot be shuttered like a bankrupt off-licence or newsagent chain, so there is always an implicit promise of state bailout in foundational activities (just as in financial services). This creates what economists would call a moral hazard because the outsourced service provider knows that, if and when things go wrong, the state's first priority will be maintaining service rather than enforcing an onerous contract.

Behind all this is the fundamental problem that the financialised parent is gaming the privilege of limited liability because on almost any measure the reciprocal relation between investor and society is being abused. The privilege that was granted to encourage equity investment has now become a means of 'de-equitising' subsidiaries: debt obligations reduce shareholder funds when special dividends are paid to the parent and wipe out the sliver of equity when things go wrong and assets are written down. This gaming shows how financialised capitalism is a system where investor/parents game institutions so as to exploit positional advantage. This has nothing to do with the practice of risk-taking entrepreneurs and the social benefits of their equity investment invoked in the rhetoric around private-sector involvement. Over-levered subsidiaries leave very little behind for society when they go bust because there are few seizable assets left once senior creditors have been paid off. Responsible equity investment leaves behind an organisation and facilities in a way that debt does not.

5.2 Veolia

The story of Veolia Environnement's incursion into UK foundational activities centres on the use of financial engineering within a complicated corporate structure. It is at one level a technical accounting story that involves an exploration of how assets are priced and money is moved around within a corporation. But it is also, at the same time, a moral story about how these accounting techniques are used to hem in profit and limit the legitimate claims of other stakeholders, dumping risk and liabilities on to UK foundational subsidiaries which benefit the French parent.

To understand the case, some background detail on the different entities within the Veolia corporate network is required. The parent company, Veolia Environnement SA, is French-owned, created by a spinoff from Vivendi in 2003 and largely bond-financed. Veolia Water UK PLC/Ltd[1] is a UK subsidiary and its main operating entity in the water utility sector. Veolia Environmental Services UK Ltd is the company's UK-based waste management arm, which is also a subsidiary of the French parent company (via various holding companies). Appendix 1 presents a simplified description of Veolia's UK corporate structure in 2010.

Veolia Environnement SA expanded its operations in the UK throughout the 2000s as it sought to take advantage of the outsourcing of council services that continued apace under New Labour. It grew both organically and by acquisition: for example, its subsidiary, Veolia Environmental Services UK, increased its revenues from just under £200m in 2000 to around £1.2bn with the acquisition of Cleanaway in 2006. But this strategy of expansion was reversed in 2011 as the Eurozone crisis led to a cyclical decline in demand for its industrial waste services and slowing profits in its core French water business (Boxell 2012). The unconsolidated accounts of the French parent also reveal large losses from its financing activities, suggesting it failed to adequately hedge interest rate and exchange rate risk as the Euro plummeted against other currencies and lending markets retrenched. As a result, Veolia's senior management announced a 5–6bn Euro divestment programme of foreign assets, the proceeds from which would be used to pay down some corporate debt, which had become a problem (Veolia Environnement SA 2011).

These divestments should, however, also be understood within the context of Veolia's use of inter-company debt and other forms of financial engineering immediately before the takeover. This began in 2010 when a fair value revaluation exercise[2] concluded that the company's assets were valued considerably below market rates. This allowed Veolia Water UK PLC to book a balance sheet revaluation surplus of £436.6m in 2010, which, through the double entry identity of the balance sheet, directly increased shareholder funds on the liability side. The quandary for Veolia was how to access the new value realised from this seemingly innocuous accounting exercise that had added hundreds of millions of pounds to its shareholder funds. Its solution was to load the subsidiary Veolia Water UK PLC with £216.9m of long-term and £108.9m of short-term inter-group loans;[3] these were then used to finance a colossal equity dividend payment of £321m to the French parent. The new inter-company debt on the balance sheet increased interest payments by £3.4m in 2010.[4] This had repercussions going forward for the UK state because interest on the group loans cannibalised the amount of taxable profit[5] (exhibit 5.1). By 2012, net interest accounted for around 40% of earnings before interest and tax, while less than 10% was paid as tax.

The asset revaluation and subsequent re-gearing effectively gave Veolia a triple gain. First, it limited the state's claim on the surpluses of the firm: the higher interest payments resulted in a lower taxable (post-interest) profit. Second, the higher interest payments retained a greater share of pre-tax profit within the corporate network. It is notable that in deteriorating market conditions, Veolia Environnement SA (the French parent) was able to step up its own dividend payout to 735.6m Euros in 2010 from 434m Euros in 2009 – an increase not too different from the sum paid to it by its UK

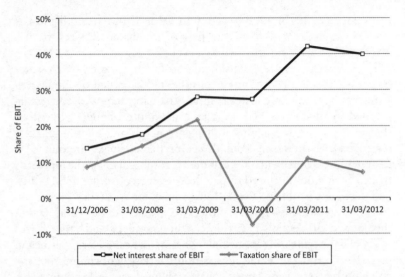

Exhibit 5.1 Veolia Water UK Limited net interest and tax share of earnings before interest and tax (EBIT)

Note 1: In 2007 Veolia Water UK Limited changed its reporting dates from December to March. Hence it only filed accounts for December 2006 and then March 2008

Note 2: The data series ends in March 2012 because, although Veolia Water UK Limited was still operating in December 2012, it was with a diminished holding of its water assets after it sold 90% of its stake in the subsidiary company in June 2012 to Affinity Water.

Source: Fame, Bureau van Dijk

subsidiary. Finally, it offered the longer-term opportunity to generate a margin spread gain if the bonds that financed the French parent had a lower average yield than the yield on group debt, effectively allowing the parent to draw income up through the subsidiaries. This financial manoeuvre would again help to displace the claims of other stakeholders like the state, or redirect cash that could have been used to fund socially useful capital investment at a time when under-investment in the water industry was being blamed for leakage and other problems.

In accounting terms, many of these effects are net neutral at the consolidated level of the French parent. The main effect is to rearrange obligations in such a manner as to squeeze other stakeholder claims at the operating level in different jurisdictions. But that changes when the subsidiaries are bought out and debts are settled. This was the case with Veolia Water Ltd in 2012 when the majority of its UK water business was sold to a consortium of investors. The deal itself was fairly complicated: first the separate licences of Veolia

Water Central Ltd (VCE), Veolia Water Southeast Ltd (VSE) and Veolia Water East Ltd (VEA) were unified and subsequently held by a holding company: Veolia Water Capital Funds Ltd (Ofwat 2012a). Veolia Water Capital Funds Ltd was then sold by Veolia Water UK PLC to a consortium led by Infracapital Partners (part of the M&G investment group, Prudential's investment arm), Beryl Datura Investment Ltd (BDIL) Equity and Morgan Stanley Infrastructure Partners. Initially the takeover vehicle was called Rift Acquisitions (Investments) Ltd (Ofwat 2012b), later becoming Affinity Water Acquisitions (Investments) Ltd on 1 October 2012. Three companies – a holdco, midco and another subsidiary – were then created between it and the bought-out Veolia Water Capital Funds Ltd (which subsequently became Affinity Water Capital Funds Ltd – see exhibit 5.2).

The financing arrangements of the deal were also complicated. On the equity side Veolia Water UK Ltd retained a 10% stake in the holdco company, with the remaining 90% stake held by Infracapital, Morgan Stanley Infrastrucure Partners and BDIL Equity. On the debt side, the buyout was financed initially through shareholder loans and £552m of bank loans (Affinity Water 2013). But within five months the loans were repaid through a new £572.9m inter-company loan, financed by a securitisation through a new Cayman Islands registered vehicle: Affinity Water Programme Finance Ltd. A further £200m from an existing bond facility was provided by Affinity Water Finance (2004) to Affinity Water Ltd acting as the guarantor (Affinity Water 2014).

The complexity of the deal worked for both sides, and the £1.2bn buyout meant particular success for the French parent, Veolia Environnement SA. First, the liabilities associated with the UK subsidiary (including the debt to finance the dividend payout in 2010) could be removed from the consolidated balance sheet. The French parent had succeeded in loading the UK operating firm with group debt to repatriate a large £321m dividend, and then had that debt taken on by the incoming investors. Second, the exit provided another opportunity for cash extraction as Veolia paid itself an additional £60m in dividends in July 2012, just as the company was sold. This was tolerable to incoming investors who in turn received £95.2m in dividends in the same year (Affinity Water Capital Funds Ltd 2013).

It is perhaps an indictment of the sector as a whole that Veolia and Affinity are often held up as exemplars of good practice in a sector awash with excessive debt and egregious special dividend payouts.

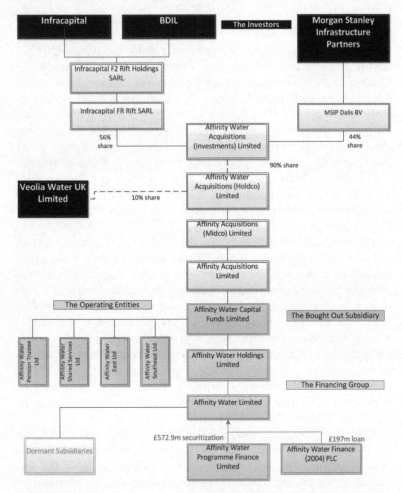

Exhibit 5.2 The corporate ownership structure of Veolia Water UK Limited
Source: Fame, Bureau van Dijk and company report and accounts

Ofwat (2013, p. 10), for example, found that regulated water companies are 'paying dividends well above those assumed in the last periodic review. At the top end of the range, companies have been paying out close to 25% of their equity asset base (equity regulatory asset value or 'RAV') to their holding companies in each year of AMP5.'⁶ But the story of Veolia's water operations tells us that even the better performing companies use and abuse inter-company loans to immure profit within the corporate network and evict the state as a claimant on its surplus, with uncertain consequences for the consumer.

Veolia used its experience in water as a template, and pulled a similar trick in its waste management subsidiary Veolia Environmental Services UK PLC, though outcomes were slightly different. Against the backdrop of declining operating profits from £44.7m in 2012 to £32.8m in 2013 as a result of declining waste volumes and rising landfill costs, the UK subsidiary Veolia Environmental Services UK PLC paid out a £300m special dividend to its French parent Veolia Environnement SA. This special dividend was again financed by a group loan which swelled net financial debt on the subsidiary's balance sheet from £171.3m in 2012 to £500.6m by the end of 2013. The balance sheet effect of adding new debt and the payment of a special dividend was to wipe £277.7m from shareholder funds. Again, the increase in interest payments as a consequence of the new debt lowered earnings before interest and tax (EBIT), meaning £6.3m less tax was returned to the exchequer compared with 2012.

Veolia Environnement SA may or may not sell off its UK waste services arm, but this 'load the donkey/flog the donkey' tactic dramatically changed the financial profile of the subsidiary. The debt-to-equity ratio ballooned in 2013 (see exhibit 5.3), which in turn reduced the book value of the firm: net assets fell from £838.1m in 2012 to £560.4m in 2013, while by our estimate, net book value fell from £453m to £181m (exhibit 5.4). Similarly the ratio of goodwill to shareholder equity, which had been falling, rose sharply to a value of two-thirds of equity funds. The importance of this should not be under-estimated, because since the introduction of the International Financial Reporting Standard 3 (IFRS3), goodwill – the difference between the market and book value of assets acquired – is no longer amortised gradually on an annual basis over a number of years, but is rather tested periodically for impairment. Goodwill is written down if it is judged that the capacity of the underlying assets to generate cash flow into the future cannot justify the current book value of these assets (European Financial Reporting Advisory Group 2014) – as we saw in Chapter 4 in the case of Serco. This raises the spectre of large, one-off write-downs if goodwill is judged to be impaired. The danger for Veolia Environmental Services UK PLC is that it is now a relatively highly levered firm operating in a difficult financial climate, just as its equity base has been deliberately eroded. It is possible that any significant impairment to goodwill could create complete financial disarray within the subsidiary with knock-on effects for delivery of service. The case of Biffa, considered in the next section, is instructive in this regard.

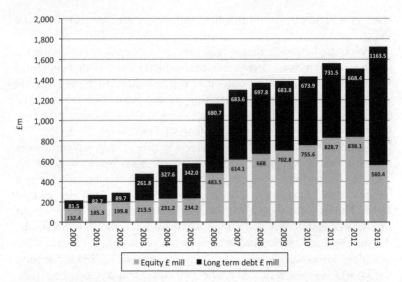

Exhibit 5.3 Veolia Environmental Services UK PLC capital structure 2000–13

Note 1: Prior to 2005 Veolia Environmental Services UK PLC was known as Onyx Environmental Group PLC

Note 2: The data series starts in 2000 because it marks a point of restructuring with an increased focus on waste management services.

Source: Company annual report and accounts, Veolia Environmental Services UK, various years

	Year end 2012	Year end 2013
	£m	£m
Tangible assets	782	877
Stock	15	15
Debtors (Short-term)	165	153
Debtors (Long-term)	954	936
Creditors (Short-term)	-629	-454
Creditors (Long-term)	-668	-1,164
Provisions	-103	-131
Net Pension Liability	-63	-51
Net Book Value	453	181

Exhibit 5.4 Estimate of Veolia Environmental Services UK PLC book value 2012 and 2013

Note: The summation of book value excludes goodwill (intangible assets)

Source: Company annual report and accounts, Veolia Environmental Services UK PLC, 2013

5.3 Biffa waste management

Biffa Ltd is the holding company for a group of companies specialising in integrated waste management services, which includes waste collection, treatment, recycling and disposal. Prior to its takeover by private equity in 2008, Biffa PLC was a stable business, earning a relatively healthy 11% profit margin and 8.6% return on capital. In April 2008 Biffa Ltd (as it became) was acquired by a private equity consortium led by Montagu Private Equity and Global Infrastructure Partners (GIP) for £1.6bn. The deal was financed almost entirely through debt from two sources: £970.4m of unsecured bank borrowings in senior and mezzanine tranches and £757.2m of unsecured, convertible inter-company debt, payable to a holding company Wasteshareholderco2, owned by the aforementioned consortium.

The stated aim of the takeover was to try to exploit the company's strong position in waste collection by investing heavily in the expansion of waste treatment and large-scale recycling facilities, to connect collection and disposal and lever gains from integration (Biffa Group Ltd 2009, p. 4). Biffa also anticipated an expansion of its energy business, which would again require investment to harness the heat produced from incinerators. Whatever the ambitions, it was abundantly clear that this type of investment would be severely restricted because the debt placed on the operating entity was so large that interest payments would swallow the money that could be used to fund capital investment. As exhibit 5.5 shows, interest payments ballooned from a manageable £23m on operating profits of £91m in 2008 to an unsustainable £176m on operating profits of £98m a year later, forcing the company into loss in 2009 after the takeover.

It may be the case that the investors simply over-estimated their ability to achieve both growth and cost reduction through reorganisation and better customer focus. But the misjudgement of operating constraints should be set in the pre-Lehman financial context of April 2008 when many private equity funds were buying firms with debt at valuations of 9 or 10 times cash flow, with the expectation of flipping them for a profit one or two years later. The buyout debt may have made the business unsustainable financially, but that was hardly the point when a 'greater fool' theory was being played out by private equity investors all over Europe who expected to make a return on the rising bull market valuations of corporate assets, passing on ever more levered corporates to the next buyer.

In this instance, however, the Lehman crisis in September 2008 meant that Montagu Private Equity and GIP were left holding the

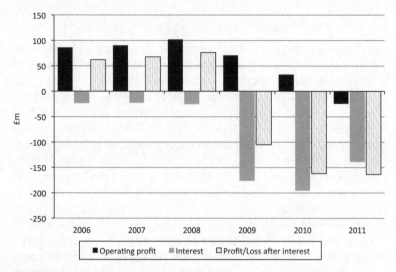

Exhibit 5.5 Biffa interest charges and operating profit

Note: Between 2009 and 2011 Biffa Group Ltd (company number 06409675) was the private equity company established to transfer the entire equity holding in Biffa Ltd (formerly Biffa PLC). The financial data for Biffa Group Ltd up to 2011 is used to illustrate how the 2009 private equity consortium acquisition of Biffa Ltd resulted in an increase in interest payments on debt that led to Biffa Group Ltd reporting a consistent loss.

Source: From 2006 to 2007 data is taken from Biffa PLC (company no. 04081901); from 2008, Biffa Ltd company number 04081901 (formerly Biffa PLC) and 2009 to 2011 data is from Biffa Group Ltd (company number 06409675)

parcel when the music stopped. Operationally, strategically and financially the company was a mess. The downturn meant landfill volumes collapsed 20% in six months (Fickling 2009) as industry and household consumption fell, leaving the company with prospects of negative growth and lots of debt. The promise of rising landfill taxes in 2013 to try to meet EU recycling targets might have encouraged socially beneficial investment in recycling capacity, but management failed to shift from landfill to recycling swiftly enough (Plimmer 2012a) because cash was eaten up by interest rather than spent on investment. This left them further exposed. Their fragile operational and financial position led to increasingly speculative, often desperate, decision making as the company could not decide whether to slim operations through a sale of its energy business (Crooks and Arnold 2010) or to expand by acquiring its rivals (Arnold 2010).

The continued disclosure of negative earnings on assets triggered a goodwill impairment assessment in 2012 which concluded that

Biffa Group Ltd would not generate sufficient future earnings to justify the goodwill sitting on its balance sheet. As a consequence it booked goodwill impairments of £729.9m in its Industrial and Commercial division and £144.8m in its Landfill and Treatment division, leaving it effectively insolvent. Wasteshareholder2, the holding vehicle for Biffa Group Ltd, was forced to convert its bond holdings of roughly £1.1bn into equity to shore up the operating company's balance sheet and maintain its solvency. With covenants breached, the company was taken over by its hedge fund lenders: Angelo Gordon, Avenue Capital Group, Babson Capital Europe and the Bain Capital affiliate Sankaty Advisors, who reduced total debt from £1.1bn to £520m and agreed to a further cash injection of £75m (Plimmer 2012b).

This is not the end of the story, because the company continues to struggle and this illustrates the difficulty of reversing under-performance quickly: in 2014 the Jersey-based holding company reported that Biffa had made accumulated losses on operations of £43m (Biffa Group Ltd 2014). Meanwhile leading analysts like Dominic Nash are sceptical as to whether the new owners' £75m additional capital investment will correct the years of under-investment (cited in Plimmer 2012b) and help build the new recycling facilities that the company – and society more generally – so desperately needs.

Biffa is not a simple story about winners, losers and egregious extraction: the private equity investors lost millions of pounds on this deal, while the creditors wrote down 45% of the value of their loans. Rather, it is a salutary tale about a private sector whose miscalculation and recklessness created mess in a foundational activity, where all stakeholders then lost out. It is also a rather sorry tale about the absence of courage and imagination on the part of our political classes whose reflex to any kind of social investment challenge is to immediately abdicate responsibility to the private sector. What was required was a model that secured steady investment for social and environmental benefit. What we got was banzai finance and disorganised activities, the chaos of which is now difficult to reverse.

5.4 Takeaways for the concerned citizen

Levering up subsidiary debt (in various ways) and extracting special dividends helps to immure profits or profit-generating assets within the corporate network at the expense of society in terms of tax

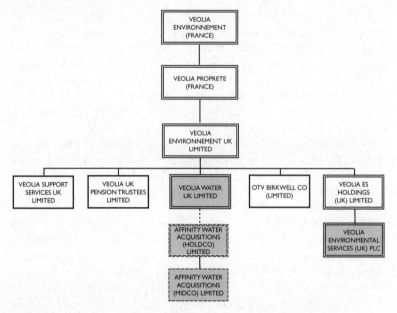

Appendix 1 The corporate ownership structure of Veolia Environnement SA

Source: Fame, Bureau van Dijk and company report and accounts

receipts paid to the exchequer. These financialised moves also create more fragile subsidiaries in foundational activities where the state has to clear up the mess when things go wrong. As citizens we are therefore effectively losing out thrice: outsourcing subsidiaries pass risk and responsibility to the state, which is offered a smaller stake in company profits, while households lose when services are not improved through productive investment. The outsourcing firms' principle of giving less and taking more breaches the principle of reciprocity that originally justified limited liability and it is time to think of alternative models of delivery in these essential services.

Notes

1 The subsidiary was named Veolia Water UK PLC until 2012; it became Veolia Water UK Ltd thereafter.
2 The revaluation exercise was as a result of Financial Reporting Standard 15 (FRS15), shifting the value of certain tangible assets from a historic cost method of valuation to a fair value assessment.
3 The asset revaluation only has a balance sheet effect (in this case significantly increasing shareholder equity on the liabilities side of the balance

sheet); the group loan was therefore used to a) re-gear the operation to balance the capital inputs of debt and equity and b) to provide the cash flow to allow the payment of a large one-off dividend to the parent (which subsequently depressed shareholder equity). Although it should be noted that the scale of the revaluation was such that shareholder equity still rose around 40% for that year.

4 Gross interest payments double, but net interest payments increase less significantly because the inter-group debt is subsequently passed on to the operating entities.

5 The share of EBIT is used as an indicator, partly to offset the effects of declining profitability more broadly as a consequence of the Eurozone fallout.

6 AMP is short for 'Asset Management Plan'. AMP5 refers to the five-year planning period for 2010–15 during which Ofwat monitored water companies' efficiency and adjusted price limits accordingly.

References

Action for Rail (2015) 'UK Commuters spend more than twice as much of their salary on fares than most European passengers'. 2 January 2015, http://actionforrail.org/uk-commuters-spend-more-than-twice-as-much-of-their-salary-on-rail-fares-than-most-european-passengers-2/ (accessed February 2015).

Adcroft, A., Haslam, C. and Williams, K. (1993) 'Leyland Daf: a good deal gone bad'. East London Business School Occasional Papers, University of East London.

Affinity Water Capital Funds Limited (2013) *Annual Report & Financial Statements for the Year Ended 31 March 2013.*

Affinity Water (2013) *Our Business Plan for 2015–2020*, December 2013. Available at: https://stakeholder.affinitywater.co.uk/docs/AW-summary-business-plan-2015–2020.pdf (accessed February 2015).

Affinity Water (2014) Affinity Water Investor Presentation, July 2014. Available at: https://stakeholder.affinitywater.co.uk/docs/Investor-Presentation.pdf (accessed March 2015).

Arnold, M. (2010) 'Biffa's owners opt to expand not sell'. *Financial Times*, 9 June 2010.

Association of Train Operating Companies (2013) *Growth and Prosperity: How Franchising Helped Transform the Railway into a British Success Story.* London: ATOC.

Ballard, M. (2012) 'Capita to cut 70 of staff in Barnet council outsourcing deal'. *ComputerWeekly.com*, 6 December 2012. Available at: http://www.computerweekly.com/news/2240173932/Capita-to-cut-70–of-staff-in-Barnet-council-outsourcing-deal (accessed February 2015).

Bamberry, C. (2012) 'Serco Group'. Peel Hunt, 1 October 2012.

Barnfield, S. (2014) 'City Council makes Service Birmingham contract available for public to read'. *Birmingham Mail*, 28 February 2014. Available at: http://www.birminghammail.co.uk/news/

midlands-news/city-council-makes-service-birmingham-6759541 (accessed April 2015).

BBC (2014) 'Jimmy Mubenga death: timeline of the case and G4S guards' trial'. *BBC News*, 16 December 2014. Available at http://www.bbc.com/news/uk-england-london-28153863 (accessed April 2015).

BBC (2015a) 'Hinchingbrooke Hospital: Circle to withdraw from contract'. 9 January 2015. Available at: http://www.bbc.co.uk/news/uk-england-cambridgeshire-30740956 (accessed March 2015).

BBC (2015b) 'Election 2015: Labour to cap private profits in NHS'. *BBC News*, 27 March 2015. Available at: http://www.bbc.com/news/election-2015–32083668 (accessed April 2015).

Bentham, J., Bowman, A., de la Cuesta, M., Engelen, E., Ertürk, I., Folkman, P., Froud, J., Johal, J., Law, J., Leaver, A., Moran, M. and Williams, K. (2013) *Manifesto for the Foundational Economy*. Working Paper 131. Manchester and Milton Keynes: CRESC. Available at: http://www.cresc.ac.uk/medialibrary/work ingpapers/wp131.pdf (accessed March 2015).

Biffa Group Ltd (2009) *Annual Report & Financial Statements*.

Biffa Group Ltd (2014) *Annual Report & Financial Statements*.

Blankenburg, S., Plesch, D. and Wilkinson, F. (2010) 'Limited liability and the modern corporation in theory and in practice'. *Cambridge Journal of Economics*, 34(5): 821–36.

Blumberg, P.I. (1986) 'Limited liability and corporate groups'. *Journal of Corporate Law*, 11: 573–631.

Booth, R. and Hopkins, N. (2012) 'Olympic security chaos: depth of G4S security crisis revealed'. *The Guardian*, 13 July 2012. Available at: http://www.theguardian.com/sport/2012/jul/12/london-2012–g4s-security-crisis (accessed April 2015).

Bowman, A., Folkman, P., Froud, J., Johal, S., Law, J., Leaver, A. and Williams, K. (2012) *Bringing Home the Bacon: From Trader Mentalities to Industrial Policy*. Manchester and Milton Keynes: CRESC. Available at: http://www.cresc.ac.uk/sites/default/files/Bringing%20home%20the%20bacon.pdf (accessed March 2015).

Bowman, A., Froud, J., Johal, S., Leaver, A. and Williams, K. (2013a) 'Opportunist dealing in the UK pig meat supply chain: trader mentalities and alternatives'. *Accounting Forum*, 37(4): 300–14.

Bowman, A., Folkman, P., Froud, J., Johal, S., Law, J., Leaver, A., Moran, M. and Williams, K. (2013b) *The Great Train Robbery: The Economic and Political Consequences of Rail Privatisation*.

Manchester and Milton Keynes: CRESC. Available at: http://www.cresc.ac.uk/sites/default/files/GTR%20Report%20final%205%20June%202013.pdf (accessed March 2015).

Bowman, A., Folkman, P., Froud, J., Johal, S., Law, J., Leaver, A., Moran, M. and Williams, K. (2013c) *The Conceit of Enterprise: Train Operators and Trade Narrative*. Manchester and Milton Keynes: CRESC. Available at: http://www.cresc.ac.uk/sites/default/files/The%20Conceit%20of%20Enterprise.pdf (accessed March 2015).

Bowman, A., Ertürk, I., Froud, J., Johal, S., Law, A., Leaver, A., Moran, M., and Williams, K. (2014) *The End of the Experiment: From Competition to the Foundational Economy*. Manchester: Manchester University Press.

Boxell, J. (2012) 'Veolia aims to cut debt as operating profits fall 25%'. *Financial Times*, 8 November 2012.

Brent, J. and Shirley, W. (2012a) 'Serco'. Liberum Capital, 28 June 2012.

Brent, J. and Shirley, W. (2012b) 'Serco expect a better H2'. Liberum Capital, 30 August 2012.

Brent, J. and Shirley, W. (2013) 'Serco results overshadowed by PECS'. Liberum Capital, 2 September 2013.

Brooke, A. (2014) 'Serco shock statement and thoughts post call'. RBC Capital Markets, 10 November 2014.

Brooke, A. and Greenall, D. (2013) 'Serco Group plc. Quantifying the uncertainties and headwinds'. RBC Capital Markets, 4 November 2013.

Brown, J.M. (2015) 'Northamptonshire Council takes outsourcing to a different level'. *Financial Times*, 12 April 2015.

Cabinet Office (2010) 'Two-tier code withdrawn'. Press release, 13 December 2010. Available at: https://www.gov.uk/government/news/two-tier-code-withdrawn (accessed March 2015).

Cameron, D. (2011) 'Speech on open public services', 11 July 2011. Available at: https://www.gov.uk/government/speeches/speech-on-open-public-services (accessed February 2015).

Cater, J. and Brown, G. (2013) 'G4S'. Canaccord Genuity, 1 July 2013.

Cater, J., Gilbert, J. and Brown, G. (2012) 'Medium-term engine for growth'. Canaccord Genuity, 14 December 2012.

Cater, J. and Woolf, S. (2014) 'Serco Group'. Numis, 12 November 2014.

Cave, A. (2015) 'How Biffa … avoided ending up on the rubbish heap'. *The Telegraph*, 11 April 2015.

Centre for Crime and Justice Studies (2013) *UK Justice Policy Review*, volume 3. http://www.crimeandjustice.org.uk/ publications/uk-justice-policy-review-volume-3 (accessed July 2014).

Chamberlain, J. (1885) Speech at Birmingham Town Hall, 5 January 1885, quoted in *The Times*, 'Mr Chamberlain at Birmingham', 6 January 1885.

Chandler, A.D. (1962) *Strategy and Structure: Chapters in the History of the American Industrial Enterprise*. Cambridge, MA: MIT Press.

Chesterton, G.K. (1927) *The Outline of Sanity*. New York: Dodd Mead and Company.

Chu, A., Foteva, S. and Sykes, T. (2013) 'A period of transition'. Deutsche Bank, 30 May 2013.

Chu, A. and Sykes, T. (2014) 'Profit warning'. Deutsche Bank, 31 January 2014.

Confederation of British Industry (CBI) (undated) *Competitive. Accountable. Transparent. A Value Driven Public Services Sector.* Available at: http://www.cbi.org.uk/media/2607468/cat_report_final.pdf (accessed March 2015).

Crooks, E. and Arnold, M. (2010) 'Biffa's landfill power unit for sale at £350m'. *Financial Times*, 6 March 2010.

Dale, P. (2013) '"Cash-strapped" Birmingham City Council paid Capita £1 billion in just six years'. *The Chamberlain Files,* 3 October 2013. http://www.thechamberlainfiles.com/cash-strapped-birmingham-city-council-paid-capita-1–billion-in-just-six-years/ (accessed April 2015).

Department for Business Enterprise and Regulatory Reform (BERR) (2008) *Understanding the Public Services Industry: How Big, How Good, Where Next? A Report by Dr DeAnne Julius.* London: BERR.

Department for Transport (DfT) (2012a) 'Cost of running the rail network'. Department for Transport. Available at: https://www.gov.uk/government/publications/cost-of-running-the-rail-network (accessed April 2015).

Department for Transport (DfT) (2012b) 'InterCity West Coast Franchise: invitation to tender'. Department for Transport. Available at: http://assets.dft.gov.uk/publications/intercity-west-coastfranchise-itt/invitation-to-tender-main-document.pdf (accessed April 2015).

Department for Transport (DfT) (2013) 'Rail franchising competi tion guide'. Department for Transport. Available at: https://www.

gov.uk/government/uploads/system/uploads/attachment_data/file/208428/franchise-competition-guide.pdf (accessed April 2015).

Dunleavy, P. (1995) 'Policy disasters: explaining the UK's record'. *Public Policy and Administration*, 10(2): 52–70.

Economist (1999) 'The key to industrial capitalism: limited liability'. *Economist*, 23 December 1999.

Elkes, N. (2014) 'Birmingham City Council's Capita call centre slammed by users'. *Birmingham Mail*, 3 October 2014. Available at: http://www.birminghammail.co.uk/news/midlands-news/birmingham-city-councils-capita-call-7877344 (accessed April 2015).

Ertürk, I., Froud, J., Johal, S., Leaver. A., Moran, M. and Williams, K. (2011) 'City state against national settlement: UK economic policy and politics after the financial crisis'. Working Paper 101, Manchester and Milton Keynes: CRESC. Available at: http://www.cresc.ac.uk/medialibrary/workingpapers/wp101.pdf (accessed March 2015).

European Financial Reporting Advisory Group (2014) *Proactive – Goodwill Impairment and Amortisation*. Available at: http://www.efrag.org/Front/p261–1–272/Proactive--Goodwill-impairment-and-amortisation.aspx (accessed February 2015).

Fickling, D. (2009) 'Waste reduction: the industry faces an uphill struggle to meet targets'. *Financial Times*, 24 April 2009.

Foteva, S. and Chu, A. (2014) 'G4S PLC'. Deutsche Bank, 15 April 2014.

Froud, J., Johal, S., Law, J., Leaver, A. and Williams, K. (2011) 'Rebalancing the economy (or buyer's remorse)'. Working Paper 87, Manchester and Milton Keynes: CRESC. Available at: http://www.cresc.ac.uk/medialibrary/workingpapers/wp87.pdf (accessed March 2015).

G4S (2014) *G4S PLC Annual Report and Accounts*.

Gash, T., Panchamia, N., Sims, S. and Hotson, L. (2013) *Making Public Service Markets Work*. London: Institute for Government.

Green, C. and Wright, O. (2015) 'Capita accused of using major government contract to short-change small companies, driving some out of business'. *The Independent*, 10 February 2015.

Green, K., Woolf, S. and Gregory, G. (2007) 'Equity research: Group 4 Securicor'. Credit Suisse, 13 November 2007.

Greenall, D. and Brooke, A. (2013) 'G4S PLC'. RBC Capital Markets, 7 May 2013.

Health Service Journal (2014) 'Serco to withdraw from UK clinical services market'. *Health Service Journal*, 15 August 2014. Available at: http://www.hsj.co.uk/news/finance/serco-to-with

draw-from-uk-clinical-services-market/5073892.article (accessed April 2015).

Heath, A. (2014) 'Serco is in a mess and only Rupert Soames can save it'. *The Telegraph*, 10 November 2014.

Hill, A. and Plimmer, G. (2013) 'G4S: the inside story'. *Financial Times*, 14 November 2013.

Hood, C. (2002) 'The risk game and the blame game'. *Government and Opposition*, 37(1): 15–37.

Hood, C. and Rothstein, H. (2001) 'Risk regulation under pressure: problem solving or blame shifting?' *Administration and Society*, 33(1): 21–53.

House of Commons Public Accounts Committee (2012) *The Ministry of Justice's Language Services Contract*. Session 2012–13. HC 620, London: The Stationery Office.

House of Commons Public Accounts Committee (2014a) *Personal Independence Payment*. Session 2013–14. HC 280, London: The Stationery Office.

House of Commons Public Accounts Committee (2014b) *Transforming Contract Management*. Session 2013–14. HC 585, London: The Stationery Office.

House of Commons Public Accounts Committee (2014c) *Contracting Out Public Services to the Private Sector*. Session 2013–14. HC 777, London: The Stationery Office.

House of Commons Work and Pensions Select Committee (2014) *Employment and Support Allowance and Work Capability Assessments*. Session 2014–15. HC 302, London: The Stationery Office.

Ireland, P. (2001) 'Defending the rentier: corporate theory and the reprivatisation of the public company' in Parkinson, J. *et al.* (eds), *The Political Economy of the Company*. Oxford: Hart Publishing: 141–73.

Ireland, P. (2010) 'Limited liability, shareholder rights and the problem of corporate irresponsibility'. *Cambridge Journal of Economics*, 34(5): 837–56.

Jee, C. (2014) 'Birmingham council to bring Capita contact centre back in-house'. *ComputerWorld UK*, 3 July 2014. Available at: http://www.computerworlduk.com/news/public-sector/3528627/birmingham-council-to-bring-capita-contact-centre-back-in-house/ (accessed April 2015).

Jenkins, K., Caines, K. and Jackson, A. (1988) *Improving Management in Government: The Next Steps*. London: Her Majesty's Stationery Office.

King, A. and Crewe, I. (2013) *The Blunders of Our Governments*. London: Oneworld Publishers.

Lee, C.H. (1986) *The British Economy Since 1700*. Cambridge: Cambridge University Press.

Lewin, J. and Burgess, K. (2014) 'FirstGroup attempts to turn corner after difficult six months'. *Financial Times*, 7 December 2014.

London Borough of Barnet (2013) 'Barnet Council and Capita sign contracts to save Barnet taxpayer millions'. News release, 6 August 2013. Available at: https://barnet.gov.uk/citizen-home/news/barnet-council-and-capita-sign-contracts-to-save-barnet-taxpayer-millions.html

Magni, A., Lloyd, M. and Kumar, R. (2013a) 'Serco Group. Downgrade to N: Contract Roulette'. HSBC, 27 February 2013.

Magni, A., Lloyd, M. and Kumar, R. (2013b) 'Flashnote: UK small and mid-cap'. HSBC, 13 March 2013.

Magni, A., Lloyd, M. and Kumar, R. (2013c) 'Company report: G4S'. HSBC, 20 May 2013.

Magni, A., Lloyd, M. and Kumar, R. (2013d) 'Company report: G4S'. HSBC, 25 October 2013.

Magni, A., Lloyd, M. and Kumar, R. (2014) 'Serco Group. When the levee breaks'. HSBC, 19 November 2014.

McCartney, S. and Stittle, J. (2011) '"Carry on up the east coast" – a case study in railway franchising'. *Public Money & Management*, 31(2): 125–9.

McKenzie, R., Vanderpump, W. and Staines, A. (2014) 'G4S: structural improvements from a secure base'. UBS, 30 June 2014.

McLoughlin, P. (2013) '20 years since rail privatisation'. Available at: https://www.gov.uk/government/speeches/20–years-since-rail-privatisation (accessed February 2015).

McLoughlin, P. (2015) Commons transport questions [Interview], 5 January 2015. Available at: http://www.publications.parliament.uk/pa/cm201415/cmhansrd/cm150105/debtext/150105-0001.htm

Middlemas, K. (1979) *Politics in Industrial Society: The Experience of the British System Since 1911*. London: Deutsch.

Milmo, D. (2006) 'GNER stripped of rail franchise over parent group's cash crisis'. *The Guardian*, 16 December 2006.

Milmo, D. (2011) 'FirstGroup may give up First Great Western franchise three years early'. *The Guardian*, 13 March 2011.

Moran, M. (2001) 'Not steering but drowning: policy catastrophes and the regulatory state'. *Political Quarterly*, 72(4): 414–27.

National Audit Office (NAO) (2003) *The Operational Performance of PFI Prisons*. London: NAO.

National Audit Office (NAO) (2013a) *The Role of Major Contractors in the Delivery of Public Services.* HC 810, London: The Stationery Office.

National Audit Office (NAO) (2013b) *Managing Government Suppliers: Report by the Comptroller and Auditor General.* HC 811, London: The Stationery Office.

National Audit Office (NAO) (2013c) *Deciding Prices in Public Services Markets: Principles for Value for Money.* London: National Audit Office.

National Audit Office (NAO) (2014) *The Ministry of Justice's Language Services Contract: Progress Update.* Session 2013–14. HC 995, London: The Stationery Office.

Odell, M. (2012) 'Government axes West Coast rail contract'. *Financial Times,* 3 October 2012.

Ofwat (2012a) 'Variation and modification of Veolia Water Central Limited's Instrument of Appointment as a Water Undertaker'. Ofwat, July 2012.

Ofwat (2012b) 'The completed acquisition of Veolia Water Capital Funds Limited by Rift Acquisitions (Investments) Limited'. Ofwat, October 2012.

Ofwat (2013) 'Observations on the regulation of the water sector'. Ofwat, 5 March 2013.

Oxford Economics (2011) *The Size of the UK Outsourcing Market.* Oxford: Oxford Economics.

Panchamia, N. (2012) *Competition in Prisons.* London: Institute for Government.

Peston, R. (2009) 'I could operate trains'. BBC News, 1 July 2009. Available at:
http://www.bbc.co.uk/blogs/thereporters/robertpeston/2009/07/i_could_operate_trains.html (accessed April 2015).

PFM (2010) 'G4S wins police forensic medical services contract'. *Premises and Facilities Management Online,* 12 August 2010. Available at: http://www.pfmonthenet.net/article/35732/G4S-wins-Police-forensic-medical-services-contract.aspx (accessed April 2015).

Pickard, J. and Adams, C. (2015) 'NMP consortium poised to lose Sellafield clean up contract'. *Financial Times,* 13 January 2015.

Plant, R., de la Grense, N. and Prior, V. (2012a) 'Serco Group'. J.P. Morgan, Cazenove, 17 February 2012.

Plant, R., de la Grense, N. and Prior, V. (2012b) 'Serco Group'. J.P. Morgan, Cazenove, 20 December 2012.

Plant, R., Sarma, A. and Prior, V (2014) 'G4S'. J.P. Morgan, Cazenove, 12 March 2014.

Plimmer, G. (2012a) 'Biffa for sale as high debt takes toll'. *Financial ~Times*, 28 March 2012.

Plimmer, G. (2012b) 'Biffa taken over by its lenders'. *Financial Times*, 29 November 2012.

Plimmer, G. (2013a) 'Outsourcing soars in public services'. *Financial Times*, 31 January 2013.

Plimmer, G. (2013b) 'G4S and Serco face criminal probe into tagging contracts'. *Financial Times*, 4 November 2013.

Plimmer, G. (2014) 'Serco chairman takes blames for crises and resigns'. *Financial Times*, 17 November 2014.

Plimmer, G. (2015a) 'Serco foots the bill for "win at all costs" public sector contracts'. *Financial Times*, 5 March 2015.

Plimmer, G. (2015b) 'Government moves to stop suppliers disclosing contract details'. *Financial Times*, 27 April 2015.

Plimmer, G., Burgess, K. and Schaefer, D. (2011) 'G4S chief admits error as ISS deal collapses'. *Financial Times*, 1 November 2011.

Plimmer, G. and Wembridge, M. (2011) 'FirstGroup to hand back rail franchise'. *Financial Times*, 11 May 2011.

Prison Officers Association (2011) *PFI Prisons – POA Briefing Paper*. London: POA.

Pound, E. (1938) *Guide to Kulchur*. London: Faber and Faber.

RBC Capital Markets (2012) 'Equity Research'. 15 August 2012.

Reed, M. (2004) 'Hudson, George [The Railway King] (1800–1871)'. *Oxford Dictionary of National Biography*. Oxford: Oxford University Press.

Reuters (2014) 'Olympic failure leaves G4S in tatters, admits CEO'. Reuters, 17 July 2014. Available at http://uk.reuters.com/article/2012/07/17/uk-oly-4gs-hearing-idUKBRE86G0AU20120717 (accessed April 2015).

Robinson, D. (2014) 'Serco finance chief to quit as group puts scandal behind it'. *Financial Times*, 16 March 2014.

Roosevelt, F.D. (1936) *Madison Square Garden Address*, 31 October 1936. Available at: http://www.presidency.ucsb.edu/ws/?pid=15219 (accessed March 2015).

Saul, J. (2007a) 'G4S'. ABN AMRO Equity Research, 13 September 2007.

Saul, J. (2007b) 'G4S'. ABN AMRO Equity Research, 28 September 2007.

Scott, J. (1998) *Seeing Like a State: How Certain Schemes to*

Improve the Human Condition Have Failed. New Haven, CT: Yale University Press.

Serco (2011) 'Serco agrees to acquire Intelenet, a leading provider of Business Process Outsourcing services to the private sector'. 31 May 2011. Available at: http://www.serco.com/media/market/bpo/intelenet.asp (accessed April 2015).

Serco (2014) 'Update on Serco's Strategy Review including the Contract & Balance Sheet Reviews; capital structure and funding; latest trading and outlook'. 10 November 2014. Available at: http://www.serco.com/Images/Serco%20SEA%2010%20Nov%202014%20-%20Updates%20on%20reviews_tcm3–45897.pdf (accessed April 2015).

Serco (2015) 'Serco Group plc – 2014 Results'. 12 March 2015. http://www.serco.com/Images/Serco%20SEA%20-%20FY14%20Results%2012%20March%202014_tcm3–46419.pdf (accessed April 2015).

Shirley, W. and Brent, J. (2011) 'Serco remarkable resilience'. Liberum Capital, 25 August 2011.

Siddique, H. (2014) 'Atos quits £500m work capability assessment contract early'. *The Guardian*, 27 March 2014.

Sturgess, G. (2012) 'The sources of benefit in prison contracting' in V. Cardwell (ed.) *Delivering Justice: The Role of the Public, Private and Voluntary Sectors in Prisons and Probation*. London: Criminal Justice Alliance.

Syal, R. (2015) 'Sellafield clean-up costs rise by £5bn in one year, says watchdog'. *The Guardian*, 4 March 2015.

Sykes, T. and Chu, A. (2009) 'G4S'. Deutsche Bank, 14 May 2008.

Thomas, N. (2014) 'FirstGroup boosted by Great Western extension'. *The Telegraph*, 9 October 2014.

Thomson (2008) 'G4S PLC interim management statement conference call'. 13 May 2008.

Thomson Reuters (2013) 'Edited transcript: G4S PLC Q3 Interim Management Statement & Capital markets Update Presentation'. 5 November 2013.

Toporowski, J. (2010) 'Corporate limited liability and the financial liabilities of firms'. *Cambridge Journal of Economics*, 34(5): 885–93.

Trade Union Congress (2013) *Justice for Sale – The Privatisation of Offender Management Services*. London: TUC.

Trade Union Congress (2015) *Towards Public Ownership* (TUC summary analysis based on Transport for Quality of Life research for Action for Rail). https://www.tuc.org.uk/sites/default/files/

TUC%20summary%20TfQL%20analysis%20March%202015_0.pdf (accessed February 2015).

Trade Union Congress and New Economics Foundation (2015) *Outsourcing Public Services*. London: TUC.

Travis, A. (2013) 'G4S contract to run sexual assault referral centres damned'. *The Guardian*, 24 May 2013.

Travis, A. (2015) 'Probation officers face redundancy'. *The Guardian*, 30 March 2015.

Unison (2011) *Time to Care: A Unison Report on Home Care*. London: Unison.

Vanderpump, W., Brandwood, J. and Liew, S. (2011) 'Serco Group PLC'. UBS, 25 August 2011.

Veolia Environnement SA (2011) 'Presentation for investor day'. Available at: http://www.finance.veolia.com/docs/Presentation-Investor-Day-2011–en.pdf (accessed February 2015).

Vickers, J. and Yarrow, G. (1991) 'Economic perspectives on privatisation'. *The Journal of Economic Perspectives*, 5(2): 111–32.

Warrell, H. (2013) 'Grayling calls for G4S and Serco revamps'. *Financial Times*, 20 August 2013.

Warrell, H. (2014) 'UK announces winners of privatised probation services contracts'. *Financial Times*, 29 October 2014.

White, A. (2013) 'Nine spectacular council outsourcing failures'. *New Statesman*, 29 August 2013. http://www.newstatesman.com/uk-politics/2013/08/nine-spectacular-council-outsourcing-failures (accessed April 2015).

Whitfield, D. (2014) *UK Outsourcing Expands Despite High Failure Rates*. Tralee: European Services Strategy Unit.